Oates

An Advent Sourcebook

D0619606

Also in the Sourcebook series:

AN ADVENT SOURCEBOOK

Edited by
Thomas J. O'Gorman

Art by
Tom Goddard

LTP
Liturgy Training Publications

Acknowledgments

The texts in this book were gathered by the editor with assistance from Gabe Huck and Peter Mazar. Texts were also received from James Burke, Evelyn Kaehler, Mary McGann and Alice Parker. We are grateful to the many publishers and authors who have given permission to include their work. Every effort has been made to determine the ownership of all texts and to make proper arrangements for their use. Any oversight that may have occurred, if brought to our attention, will gladly be corrected in future editions.

Acknowledgment for the sources not listed below will be found in the endnotes.

Scripture texts used in this work, unless otherwise noted, are taken from the *New American Bible with Revised New Testament,* copyright ©1986 Confraternity of Christian Doctrine, and are used by license of copyright owner. All rights reserved. No part of *The New American Bible with Revised New Testament* may be reproduced in any form without permission in writing from the copyright owner.

Editorial assistant: Theresa Pincich.
Production: Jane Caplan, Phyllis Martinez, Julianne Clark.
Series design format: Michael Tapia

Copyright ©1988, Archdiocese of Chicago: Liturgy Training Publications, 1800 North Hermitage Avenue, Chicago IL 60622-1101; 1-800-933-1800; FAX 1-800-933-7094. All rights reserved.

Printed in the United States of America.

ISBN 0-930467-82-5
ADVENT

Contents

Introduction

THE SEASON OF ADVENT resets the clocks and calendars of Christian worship. Annually, we leap into another gospel tradition and maneuver into a familiar yet foggy cycle. Sounds and signs of dubious direction surround us. Slipper and pajama sizes, not the quiet beauty of our noble tradition, often preoccupy us. We are easily left with the shallow, the cliché. This *Advent Sourcebook* is offered as life buoy, antidote, prayer book, literary catalog of tradition. It is all of this for parents, presiders, pastors, preachers, teachers, believers who want to peel back a tad more of Advent's many-layered meaning.

The poetry, parable, song, scripture and story contained here attempt to broaden and stretch the rhythms and motions of the Advent season. These texts set out to arouse our imagination and our awareness for what Advent's time brings: a mature expectation and sensitivity to the Lord's coming. The curious juxtaposing of these texts offers new perceptions about the substance from which this season is made. Intersecting here are the verities of many cultures, customs, theologies and literatures. How they collide and interact draws wide margins for the mystery they seek to articulate.

Advent summons us to the beginning. The lavishness of God's compassion and mercy frame yet another year for us. With the arrival of Advent's first Sunday, we attend to this mystery one more time. Clearly, we are a people whose origins and destiny make us curious yet apprehensive about the day of the Lord's coming. Our tradition proclaims this as both an event already accomplished in human history and an event moving toward fulfillment in the future—our future. Our worship, fashioned of word and sacrament, insists that our encounter with the day of the Lord occurs concretely in the struggles and tensions, choices and decisions of human living. Through the ages, poets, teachers, storytellers, mystics, rabbis, saints, political activists and martyrs for the justice of the gospel—all these, most of them ordinary people, have handed on to us words and images that identify and describe this encounter with the day of the Lord. They tell us about it as present reality and yet to come. Their words create a literature that lifts up this season of readiness for the advent of God in our living.

The drama and adventure that this *Sourcebook* catalogs can echo against our personal rhythm in prayer and worship and living. Thus, little by little, we ripen, mature in our preparation for the celebration of the nativity and our preparation for the glory of another coming. Advent is a multilayered season of meanings. Over and over, we find ourselves centered in the extravagant documentation that spells out God's penchant for wonder, mystery and surprise. Perhaps we will discover ourselves hungry for more. Beneath the predictable commotion of this season we might catch the sense of things so ancient and so new, so intimate and so shattering.

This book may be used in many ways. Its movement is that of Advent itself, but Advent is different each year and every Advent will bring its own order to these pages. The few words that identify the sections in the table of contents, and that run along the top of each page, are guides to the texts themselves. These words show the season unfolding as they name some of the holy people we remember in Advent or announce one of the images that identifies Advent. Though the book is meant to assist preachers and musicians and all who prepare or minister at the liturgy, its primary work is to nourish the prayer and reflection of any person who keeps this season. Read from these pages each day, perhaps within a simple morning or evening prayer, or at table, or with the lighting of the Advent wreath.

The rhythms in these words carry us deeper into the colors and melodies of Advent. They unleash better ritual, better humor, better vigilance. If these texts also widen the bounds of our literacy, then we are doubly blessed.

Thanks must go to the thinkers and writers and speakers whose words spring up here. Thanks also to Gloria Sieben and the staff of Mundelein Seminary Library for their access to sources and their endless kindness. Thanks to Ida Abernathy and the staff of the Poetry Center, University of Arizona, Tucson, for their helpfulness and welcome.

Finally, to Colette and Lou Briody to whom this work is dedicated: for you my heart always gives thanks. Because of you I wait with more excitement for the One whose coming is certain.

Thomas J. O'Gorman

CONDITOR alme siderum,
Aeterna lux credentium,
Christe Redemptor omnium,
Exaudi preces supplicum:

Qui condolens interitu
Mortis perire saeculum,
Salvasti mundum languidum,
Donans reis remedium,

Vergente mundi vespere,
Uti sponsus de thalamo,
Egressus honestissima
Virginis matris clausula.

Cujus forti potentiae
Genu curvantur omnia
Caelestia, terrestria,
Nutu fatentur subdita.

Te deprecamur, hagie,
Venture judex saeculi,
Conserva nos in tempore
Hostis a telo perfidi.

Evening hymn
for Advent
Eighth century

CREATOR of the stars of night,
Your people's everlasting light,
O Christ, Redeemer of us all,
We pray you hear us when we call.

In sorrow that the ancient curse
Should doom to death a universe,
You came, O Savior, to set free
Your own in glorious liberty.

Come, Sun and Savior, to embrace
Our gloomy world, its weary race,
As groom to bride, as bride to groom:
The wedding chamber, Mary's womb.

At your great Name, O Jesus, now
All knees must bend, all hearts must bow;
All things on earth with one accord,
Like those in heav'n, shall call you Lord.

Come in your holy might, we pray,
Redeem us for eternal day;
Defend us while we dwell below,
From all assaults of our dread foe.

Evening hymn
for Advent
Eighth century

F OR many, Advent would not be Advent if introduced by
any other hymn. It is well-nigh impossible for even the
best of poets to find a formula that really corresponds to the
first line of the Latin text. The Latin "sidus" ["siderum"]
means more than "star." It includes the stars, of course, but
also sun and moon and planets and all the heavenly constel-
lations and comets and meteors. These are the cosmic
elements that will appear in later stanzas of the hymn. For
the ancients, these mysterious heavenly bodies that moved
about and that had their cycles of waxing and waning and
that in some unfathomable way could affect the course of
human destiny—these heavenly bodies were perhaps living
beings.

The opening line of this Advent hymn should make us think
of the great array of all the powerful cosmic bodies that
figure in those eschatological texts of scripture where the
whole of the created universe responds to the presence of its
God. The point of reference is not some lovely nightfall
scene studded with gently glimmering stars, but rather that
Great Day when "the sun will be darkened, and the moon

will not give her light, the stars will fall from heaven, and the powers of heaven will be shaken" (Matthew 24:29). Indeed, this Advent hymn, if we really look at it, is something of a "Dies irae" in a less strident mode.

In stanza three, the world's evening draws to a close. We recognize in the last three lines of this stanza the allusion to verse six of Psalm 19, the verse that occurs so frequently in the Christmastide cycle: "And he, as a bridegroom coming forth from the bridal chamber, rejoices as a giant to run his course." So just when the world seems doomed to certain extinction, the Sun comes forth in a blaze of light and begins its paschal journey across the whole of human life and experience. This imagery is especially appropriate towards the beginning of December and the first Sunday of Advent, when nights are growing progressively longer and longer, until, upon the arrival of the winter solstice just before Christmas, the inexorable onslaught of darkness is reversed with the birth of Christ, the Sun of Justice, who now begins to run his course over the whole of our existence.

Chrysogonus Waddell

WHEN the Man of Heaven comes in his glory, and all the angels with him, then he will sit on his glorious throne. Before him will be gathered all the nations, and he will separate them one from another as a shepherd separates the sheep from the goats, and he will place the sheep at his right hand, but the goats at the left. Then the king will say to those at his right hand, "Come, O blessed of my Father, inherit the realm prepared for you from the foundation of the world; for I was hungry and you gave me food, I was thirsty and you gave me drink, I was a stranger and you welcomed me, I was naked and you clothed me, I was sick and you visited me, I was in prison and you came to me." Then the righteous will answer him, "Lord, when did we see you hungry and feed you, or thirsty and give you drink? And when did we see you a stranger and welcome you, or naked and clothe you? And when did we see you sick or in prison and visit you?" And the king will answer them, "Truly, I say to you, as you did to one of the littlest of these my dear people, you did it to me." Then the king will say to those at his left hand, "Depart from me, you cursed, into the eternal fire prepared for the devil and the devil's angels; for I was hungry and you gave me no food, I was thirsty and you gave me no drink, I was a stranger and you did not welcome me, naked and you did not clothe me, sick and in prison and you did not visit me." Then they also will answer, "Lord, when did we see you hungry or thirsty or a stranger or naked or sick or in prison, and did not minister to you?" Then he will answer them, "Truly, I say to you, as you did it not to one of the littlest of these, you did it not to me." And they will go away into eternal punishment, but the righteous into eternal life.

Matthew 25:31–46

A DVENT is both a beginning and an end, an alpha and an omega of the church's year of grace. Too often considered merely a season of preparation for the annual commemoration of Christ's birth, this rich and many-layered season is actually designed to prepare the Christian for the glorious possibilities of the parousia. It is a season of longing expectation—"Come, Lord Jesus" (Revelation 22:20).

William G. Storey

A DVENTUS" is the exact Christian Latin equivalent of the Greek "parousia."

H. A. Reinhold

W ITH inward pain my heartstrings sound,
      My soul dissolves away;
Dear Sovereign, whirl the seasons round,
Dear Sovereign, whirl the seasons round,
And bring, and bring the promised day,
And bring the promised day.

Early American hymn

N OBODY knows exactly how Advent started, but the custom is very ancient. In his *History of the Franks*, St. Gregory of Tours wrote that one of his predecessors, St.

Perpetuus, who held the see around 480, decreed a fast three times a week from the feast of St. Martin, November 11, until Christmas. In 567, the Second Council of Tours enjoined monks to fast from the beginning of December until Christmas. This penance was soon extended to the laity and was pushed back to begin on St. Martin's Day. This 45-day Advent was nicknamed "St. Martin's Lent." From France the practice of doing penance during Advent spread to England as is noted in Venerable Bede's history.

Hubert Dunphy

E XCITA, quaesumus Domine, potentiam tuam, et veni. Summon all your strength, O Lord, and come.

Roman liturgy

O UR time is a time of waiting; waiting is its special destiny. And every time is a time of waiting, waiting for the breaking in of eternity. All time runs forward. All time, both history and in personal life, is expectation. Time itself is waiting, waiting not for another time, but for that which is eternal.

Paul Tillich

W INTER wakeneth all my care;
    Now when leaves waxeth bare,
Oft I sigh and sorrow sore
    When it cometh into my thought
Of this world's joy, how it goeth all to nought.

Now it is, and now it is gone,
    As if it had never been.
What many say, sooth it is:
    All goeth but God's will!
All shall die, though we like it nil!

All that grows forth into dust,
    Now it fadeth all at once:

Jesu! Help that it be seen,
    And shield us from hell!
Fourteenth century For I know not whither I go, nor how long I here dwell.

PASSING away, saith the World, passing away:
    Chances, beauty and youth, sapped day by day:
Thy life never continueth in one stay.
Is the eye waxen dim, is the dark hair changing to grey
That hath won neither laurel nor bay?
I shall clothe myself in Spring and bud in May:
Thou, root-stricken, shalt not rebuild thy decay
On my bosom for aye.
Then I answered: Yea.

Passing away, saith my Soul, passing away:
With its burden of fear and hope, of labour and play,
Hearken what the past doth witness and say:
Rust in thy gold, a moth is in thine array,
A canker is in thy bud, thy leaf must decay.
At midnight, at cockcrow, at morning, one certain day
Lo the Bridegroom shall come and shall not delay,
Watch thou and pray.
Then I answered: Yea.

Passing away, saith my God, passing away:
Winter passeth after the long delay:
New grapes on the vine, new figs on the tender spray,
Turtle calleth turtle in Heaven's May.
Though I tarry, wait for Me, trust Me, watch and pray:
Arise, come away, night is past and lo it is day.
Christina Rossetti
Nineteenth century My love, My sister, My spouse, thou shalt hear Me say.
Then I answered: Yea.

I N illa die stillabunt montes dulcedinem,
et colles fluent lac et mel.

On that day the mountains will stream with sweetness
and the hills will flow with milk and honey.   Monastic liturgy

B ELOVED, now is the acceptable time spoken of by the
Spirit, the day of salvation, peace and reconciliation:
the great season of Advent. This is the time eagerly awaited
by the patriarchs and prophets, the time that holy Simeon
rejoiced to see. This is the season that the church has always
celebrated with special solemnity. We too should always
observe it with faith and love, offering praise and thanksgiv-
ing to the Father for the mercy and love he has shown us in   Charles Borromeo
this mystery.   Sixteenth century

L OVE is most nearly itself
When here and now cease to matter.
Old men ought to be explorers
Here and there does not matter
We must be still and still moving
into another intensity
For a further union, a deeper communion
Through the dark cold and the empty desolation,
The wave cry, the wind cry, the vast waters
Of the petrel and the porpoise. In my end is my
    beginning.   T. S. Eliot

T HERE is an appointed time for everything,
and a time for every affair under the heavens.
A time to be born, and a time to die;
a time to plant, and a time to uproot the plant.
A time to weep, and a time to laugh;
a time to mourn, and a time to dance.   Ecclesiastes 3:1–2, 4

William Blake
Eighteen century

ETERNITY is in love with the production of time.

How sour sweet music is
When time is broke and no proportion kept!
So is it in the music of men's lives.
And here have I the daintiness of ear
To check time broke in a disorder'd string:
But, for the concord of my state and time,
Had not an ear to hear my true time broke.
I wasted time, and now doth time waste me.

William Shakespeare
Sixteenth century

Time, that anticipates eternities
And has an art to resurrect the rose;
Time, whose last siren song at evening blows
With sun-flushed cloud shoreward on toppling seas;
Time, arched by planets lonely in the vast
Sadness that darkens with the fall of day;
Time, unexplored elysium; and grey
Death-shadow'd pyramid that we have named the past—
Magnanimous Time, patient with man's vain glory;
Ambitious road; Lethe's awaited guest;
Time, hearkener to the stumbling passionate story
Of human failure humanly confessed;
Time, on whose stair we dream our hopes of heaven,

Sigfried Sassoon

Help us to judge ourselves, and so be shriven.

A DVENT is the time for rousing. We are shaken to the very depths, so that we may wake up to the truth of ourselves. The primary condition for a fruitful and rewarding Advent is renunciation, surrender. We must let go of all our mistaken dreams, our conceited poses and arrogant gestures, all the pretenses with which we hope to deceive ourselves and others. If we fail to do this, stark reality may take hold of us and rouse us forcibly in a way that will entail both anxiety and suffering.

Alfred Delp

A BBA John the Little said: We have abandoned a light burden, namely self-criticism, and taken up a heavy burden, namely self-justification.

Desert Wisdom

T HE day after Thanksgiving the *New York Times* told of a 33-year-old local cab driver whose shoulder-length hair was tied in a ponytail. (Don't get distracted by the ponytail!) About five years ago, this cabby "prayed to God for guidance on how to help the forgotten people of the streets who exist in life's shadows." As he recalls it, God replied: "Make eight pounds of spaghetti, throw it in a pot, give it out on 103rd Street and Broadway with no conditions, and people will come." He did, they came, and now he goes from door to door giving people food to eat.

I am not asking you to stuff the Big Apple with spaghetti. But a New York cabby can bring light into your Advent night. He prayed to a God who was there; he listened; he gave the simple gift God asked of him; he gave "with no conditions"; and people responded. Here is your Advent: Make the Christ who has come a reality, a living light, in your life and in some other life. Give of yourself . . . to one dark soul . . . with no conditions.

Walter J. Burghardt

W HAT happened to marriage and family that it should
have become a travail and a sadness? . . . God may
be good, family and marriage and children and home may
be good, grandma and grandpa may act wise, the Thanksgiving table may be groaning with God's goodness and
bounty, all the folks healthy and happy, but something is
missing. . . . What is missing? Where did it go? I won't have
it! I won't have it! Why this sadness here? Don't stand for it!
Get up! Leave! Let the boat people sit down! Go live in a
cave until you've found the thief who is robbing you. But at
Walker Percy   least protest. Stop, thief! What is missing? God? Find him!

T HE reign of God, the eschatological liberation of the
world, is already in process, is already being estab-
Leonardo Boff   lished. It takes shape in concrete modifications of actual life.

A S to the times and the seasons, my dear people, you
have no need to have anything written to you. For you
yourselves know well that the day of the Lord will come like
a thief in the night. When people say, "There is peace and
security," then sudden destruction will come upon them as
labor pangs come upon a woman with child, and there will
be no escape. But you are not in darkness, my dear people,
for that day to surprise you like a thief. For you are all
children of light and children of the day; we are not of the
night or of darkness. So then let us not sleep, as others do,
but let us keep awake and be sober. For those who sleep
sleep at night, and those who get drunk are drunk at night.
But, since we belong to the day, let us be sober, and put on
the breastplate of faith and love, and for a helmet the hope of
salvation. For God has not destined us for wrath, but to
obtain salvation through our Lord Jesus Christ, who died for
us so that whether we wake or sleep we might live with him.
Therefore encourage one another and build one another up,
1 Thessalonians 5:1–11   just as you are doing.

B RIGHT mornin' stars are risin',
Bright mornin' stars are risin',
Bright mornin' stars are risin',
   Day is a-breakin' in my soul.

Oh where are our dear fathers?
   Oh where are our dear mothers?
Oh where are sisters and brothers?
Day is a-breakin' in my soul.

Some are down in the valley prayin',
   Some are deep in the mountain sleepin',
Some are up in heaven shoutin',
   Day is a-breakin' in my soul.

*Appalachian
folk hymn*

A BBA Poemen said about Abba Pior that every single day
he made a fresh beginning.

Desert Wisdom

D ARKNESS provides us with a therapeutic limit-experi-
ence, illuminating the meagerness of human re-
sources for experiencing, understanding and communica-
ting the divine. It reminds us that God alone has an adequate
idea of who God is and that even our most successful efforts
at understanding God are inadequate. When darkness
induces modesty, humility, faith and trust, it leads to a
communion with God as God really is; it frees us from the
self-deception of worshiping gods of our own making. Only
the real God saves; not the illusion. The true Israelite is the
wise person who makes a home "in the shadow of the
Shaddai" (Psalm 91:1).

John Navone

ADVENT then is dedicated to the last things, to death, judgment, heaven and hell, but above all to Jesus' glorious coming to complete his Easter work. The church goes so far as to set aside an entire liturgical season to the end of the world and the final coming of the Lord, so important a part of the faith does she consider these truths.

Charles K. Riepe

COME, and make all things new,
Build up this ruined earth;
Restore our faded paradise,
Creation's second birth!

Horatius Bonar
Nineteenth century

TO you, O Lord, I give my life;
You are my God.
I trust you; you will not shame me;
Do not let my enemies gloat at my downfall!
Do not disappoint those who wait for you,
But let the treacherous come to grief.

Make me know your paths, O Lord;
And teach me your ways.
Teach me to walk by faith in you,
For you are the God who saves me.
I wait for you eagerly all day long,
Because of your goodness, O Lord.

Remember your mercy and gracious love—
The qualities you have always had.
Forget my youthful rebellions and sins;
Remember me as one whom you love.

The Lord is just and good,
And teaches sinners the way,
Guiding humble people to justice,
And showing them how to find it.

Lord, act with eternal kindness
Toward those who keep your covenant.
For the sake of your name, O Lord,
Forgive my sin, great as it is.

Will you not teach your chosen way
To all who worship you?
Let them sleep knowing all is well;
Let their children possess the world.
O Lord, counsel those who fear you,
And teach them your covenant.   Psalm 25:2–14

W HEN we handle the sick and the needy we touch the
   suffering body of Christ and this touch will make us
heroic; it will make us forget the repugnance and natural
tendencies in us. We need the eyes of deep faith to see Christ
in the broken body and dirty clothes under which the most
beautiful one among us hides. We shall need the hands of
Christ to touch these bodies wounded by pain and suffering.

Mother Teresa
of Calcutta

A FTER 1976 Dorothy [Day] virtually withdrew from the
   affairs of the world of the Worker movement. Her lot, as
she knew, was to await death. Content to spend as much
time as she could in the company of her daughter and
grandchildren, she remained in her room at Maryhouse,
coming downstairs only for the evening Mass that was said at
the house. In her room, which overlooked Third Street, she
could look out onto the dismal prospect of a narrow street,
shadowed by five-story buildings, shoulder to shoulder,
whose unkempt and desolate appearance suggested that
they, like the people who passed before them, felt that their

existence mattered not at all. In front of these buildings, parked cars at the curbs were jammed against one another. One structure, ugly with shattered windows and an aspect of grotesque garishness, was fronted by motorcycles—powerful brutish machines with signs and symbols that proclaimed their owners' defiance of civilized norms. The building was the home of the Hell's Angels, a motorcycle gang about whose doings fearful stories were told.

It was in this part of New York that Dorothy had spent a half-century of her life, where just blocks away she had lived in 1917 as the acting editor of the *Masses* and where in that cold winter of 1918 she had whiled away the nights with Eugene O'Neill and the young radicals and artists of the Village. A few blocks to the west and south was New York's Lower East Side, the home of the Jews. She had never left them. Mott Street was two blocks away, the street of the Italians. She remembered sitting on the front steps of the Mott Street house, watching them celebrate the feast of San Gennaro. Perhaps she remembered that night soon after the war had begun, the cool clear air and the half-moon shining brightly over Mott Street. . . .

Dorothy died on November 29, 1980, just as night began to soften the harshness of the poverty and ugliness of Third Street. Her daughter, Tamar, was in the room with her. There was no struggle. The last of the energy that sustained her life had been used.

The funeral was on December 2 at the Nativity Catholic Church, a half block away from Maryhouse. An hour before the service, scheduled for 11 o'clock in the morning, people began to assemble in the street. Some were curious onlookers, the hollow-eyed and stumbling people who roam the streets of lower New York, but others were drawn there by some sense of the propriety of paying their last respects to the woman who had clothed and fed them. There were American Indians, Mexican workers, blacks and Puerto Ricans. There were people in eccentric dress, apostles of causes who had felt a great power and truth in Dorothy's life. . . .

At the appointed time, a procession of these friends and fellow workers came down the sidewalk. At the head of it Dorothy's grandchildren carried the pine box that held her body. Tamar, Forster, and her brother John followed. At the church door, Cardinal Terence Cooke met the body to bless it. As the procession stopped for this rite, a demented person pushed his way through the crowd and bending low over the coffin peered at it intently. No one interfered, because, as even the funeral directors understood, it was in such as this man that Dorothy had seen the face of God.   William D. Miller

A LICE Paul, the suffragist leader, had gold pins made, depicting prison bars, to give to those who went to jail with her in the second decade of this century. Dorothy Day was given one of those pins; but I would bet she did not have it when she died this week. She was not good at owning things. She was good at giving things away, including herself. It is the only way, finally, to own oneself.

In her own and this century's teens she was an ardent defender of other people's rights. She continued to speak up for the unprotected when no one else would do that. During World War II, her protests at the internment without due process of Japanese-Americans caused J. Edgar Hoover to open his extensive file on her. Without her, how much bleaker would be our record. She fed the poor, which may not be the Christian's final task, but should normally be the first one.

She was the long-distance runner of protest in our time, because her agitation was built on serenity, her activism on contemplation, her earthly indignation on unearthly trust. This or that cause, with its noisy followers, came and went, but she was always there. "Rest in peace," one prays over the dead; but she reposed in restlessness, so long as there was no peace—and her moral discontent should be continued. Let her rest in our disquietude.

Dorothy Day showed us . . . that people who stand with and for others cannot act from a calculus of individual advantage. They must act as they do from a higher urgency, a love beyond what most of us think of as loving. So far from distracting them from earth's injustice, as Marx claimed religion did, Dorothy Day's faith made effective radicalism not only possible, for many people, but imperative. We may not even be able to possess the earth unless we aspire to heaven—like our sister, who is dead and lives.

Garry Wills

A brother said to an old man: There were two brothers. One of them stays in his cell quietly, fasting for six days at a time, and imposing on himself a good deal of discipline, and the other serves the sick. Which one of them is more acceptable to God? The old man replied: Even if the brother who fasts six days were to hang himself by the nose, he could not equal the one who serves the sick.

Desert Wisdom

IN each of our lives Jesus comes as the bread of life—to be eaten, to be consumed by us. This is how he loves us. Then Jesus comes in our human life as the hungry one, the other, hoping to be fed with the bread of our life, our hearts loving, and our hands serving. In loving and serving, we prove that we have been created in the likeness of God, for God is love and when we love we are like God. This is what Jesus meant when he said, "Be perfect as your Father in heaven is perfect."

Mother Teresa
of Calcutta

THIS morning to ward off the noise I have my radio on— Berlioz, Schubert, Chopin, etc. It is not a distraction, it is a pacifier. As St. Teresa of Avila said as she grabbed her castanets and started to dance during the hour of recreation in her unheated convent, "One must do something to make life bearable!"

Dorothy Day

I feel that all families should have the conveniences and comforts which modern living brings and which do simplify life, and give time to read, to study, to think, and to pray. And to work in the apostolate, too. But poverty is my vocation, to live as simply and poorly as I can, and never to cease talking and writing of poverty and destitution. Here and everywhere. "While there are poor, I am of them. While men are in prison, I am not free," as Debs said and as we often quote.

Dorothy Day

A NDREW the apostle, the brother of Peter, was born at Bethsaida, a town of Galilee. He was one of the disciples of John the Baptist and heard him say of Christ, "Behold the Lamb of God." Immediately he followed Jesus, bringing his brother also with him. After Christ's death and resurrection, the province of Scythia was allotted to Andrew as the place of his preaching. After working there, he went through Epirus and Thrace and converted multitudes to Christ by his teaching and miracles.

Finally he went to Patras in Achaia, and there likewise he converted many to the knowledge of the gospel. He fearlessly rebuked Aegeas, the proconsul, who opposed the preaching of the gospel, because he who wished to be considered as a judge of others was himself so deceived by the devil as not to know the judge of all, Christ the Lord. Filled with anger, Aegeas answered him: "Boast no more of your Christ. He spoke as you do but his words did not help him, for he was crucified." Andrew boldly answered that Christ had delivered himself for the salvation of humankind, but he was insultingly interrupted by the proconsul and told to look out for himself and to sacrifice to the gods. Andrew then replied: "We have an altar on which I offer up to God every day, not the flesh of bulls nor the blood of goats, but a spotless Lamb; and when all the faithful have eaten the flesh thereof, this Lamb that was slain remains whole and lives."

Aegeas was then filled with anger and sent the apostle, bound, to prison. The people would have set him free, but he calmed them and begged of them not to take away from him the palm of martyrdom which he so much desired and which now was within reach. Shortly thereafter he was brought before the judgment seat where he extolled the mystery of the cross and rebuked Aegeas for his impiety. Aegeas, not being able to bear with him any longer, commanded him to be crucified as was Christ.

Andrew was then led to the place of martyrdom, and as soon as he saw the cross he cried out, "O precious cross, which the members of my Lord have made so honorable, how long have I desired you! How fervently I have loved you! How constantly I have sought you! And now that you have come to me, how my soul is attracted to you. Take me from here and unite me to my master, that as by you he redeemed me, so by you also he may take me to himself." Then he was fastened to the cross, where he continued to live for two days, not ceasing to preach the faith of Christ. Finally he passed into the presence of him, the likeness of whose death he had loved so well.

Monastic office of readings

B LESSED feasts of blessed martyrs,
Holy women, holy men,
With affection's recollections
Greet we your return again.

*Latin hymn
Twelfth century*

T HE next day John was there again with two of his disciples, and as he watched Jesus walk by, he said, "Behold, the Lamb of God." The two disciples heard what he said and followed Jesus. Jesus turned and saw them following him and said to them, "What are you looking for?" They said to him, "Rabbi" (which translated means Teacher), "where are you staying?" He said to them, "Come, and you will see." So they went and saw where he was staying, and they stayed with him that day. It was about four in the afternoon. Andrew, the brother of Simon Peter, was one of the two who heard John and followed Jesus.

John 1:38–40

THERE are so many deaths everywhere that it is incredible.

The "death squadron" strikes in so many poor homes. A family of seven, including three small children, was machine-gunned to death in a nearby town just last week. It is a daily thing—death and bodies found everywhere, many decomposing or attacked by animals because no one can touch them until they are seen by a coroner. It is an atmosphere of death.

The organized, as they call the left, are made up of some of those simple courageous, suffering farmers. In the Pastoral de Asistencia [Pastoral Assistance] work that Ita began in Chatelango, one comes in contact with so many poor refugees—women and children especially, who have lost husbands, brothers, fathers.

It has become an ordinary daily happening. Two lovely young women were cut into pieces by machetes in a community nearby where so many of the people have been killed. The brave mother of one of these young women is also the mother-in-law of the other and she was here with us taking refuge. We are trying to help the refugees—bringing them to shelters and getting food to places where it is desperately needed.

Archbishop Romero [murdered while he said Mass in San Salvador on March 23] and all the martyrs of this little violent land must be interceding for a new day for Salvador.

I am beginning to see death in a new way, dearest Katie. For all these precious men, women, children struggling in just laying down their lives as victims, it is surely a passageway to *life* or, better, a change of life. . . .

I don't know what tomorrow will bring. I am at peace here and searching—trying to learn what the Lord is asking. Ita is a beautiful, faith-filled young woman. I am learning much from her. At this point, I would hope to be able to go on, God willing. . . . This seems what he is asking of me at this moment. The work is really what Archbishop Romero called "acompañamiento" [accompanying the people], as well as searching for ways to bring help.

Write to me soon. Know that I love you and pray for you daily. Keep us in your heart and prayers, especially the poor forsaken people.

Maura Clarke

Maura Clarke was a Maryknoll sister working with the poor in El Salvador when she wrote this letter in October 1980. On December 2, Maura Clarke, Ita Ford, Jean Donovan and Dorothy Kazel were brutally murdered.

A RCHBISHOP Romero offers her a chair. Marianela prefers to talk standing up. She always comes for others, but this time Marianela comes for herself. Marianela García Vilas, attorney for the tortured and disappeared of El Salvador, does not come this time to ask the archbishop's solidarity with one of the victims of D'Aubuisson, Captain Torch, who burns your body with a blowtorch, or of some other military horror specialist. Marianela doesn't come to ask help for anyone else's investigation or denunciation. This time she has something personal to say to him. As mildly as she can, she tells him that the police have kidnapped her, bound, beat, humiliated, stripped her—and that they raped her. She tells it without tears or agitation, with her usual calm, but Archbishop Romero has never before heard in Marianela's voice these vibrations of hatred, echoes of disgust, calls for vengeance. When Marianela finishes, the archbishop, astounded, falls silent too.

After a long silence, he begins to tell her that the church does not hate or have enemies, that every infamy and every action against God forms part of a divine order, that criminals are also our brothers and must be prayed for, that one must forgive one's persecutors, one must accept pain, one must . . . Suddenly, Archbishop Romero stops.

He lowers his glance, buries his head in his hands. He shakes his head, denying it all, and says: "No, I don't want to know."

"I don't want to know," he says, and his voice cracks.

Archbishop Romero, who always gives advice and comfort, is weeping like a child without mother or home. Archbishop Romero, who always gives assurances, the tranquilizing assurance of a neutral God who knows all and embraces all—Archbishop Romero doubts.

Romero weeps and doubts and Marianela strokes his head.   Eduardo Galeano

T AKE heed, watch; for you do not know when the time will come. It is like someone going on a journey, who leaving home and putting the servants in charge of their work, commands the doorkeeper to be on the watch. Watch therefore—for you do not know when the lord of the house will come, in the evening, or at midnight, or at cockcrow, or in the morning—lest the lord come suddlenly and find you asleep. And what I say to you I say to all: Watch.   Mark 13:33–37

Y OU, O LORD, are father to us,
    our Redeemer from of old is your name.
O LORD, why do you make us err from your ways
    and harden our heart, so that we fear you not?
Return for the sake of your servants,
    the tribes of your heritage.
O that you would rend the heavens and come down,
    that the mountains might quake at your presence—
as when fire kindles brushwood
    and the fire causes water to boil—
to make your name known to your adversaries,
    and that the nations might tremble at your presence!

When you did terrible things which we looked not for,
  you came down, the mountains quaked
    at your presence.
From of old no one has heard
  or perceived by the ear,
no eye has seen a God besides you,
  who works for those who await you.
You meet those who joyfully work righteousness,
  those who remember you in your ways.
Behold, you were angry, and we sinned;
  in our sins we have been a long time,
    and shall we be saved?
We have all become like one who is unclean,
  and all our righteous deeds are like a polluted garment.
We all fade like a leaf,
  and our iniquities, like the wind, take us away.
There is no one that calls upon your name,
  who arises to take hold of you;
for you have hid your face from us,
  and have delivered us into the hand of our iniquities.
Yet, O LORD, you are father to us;
  we are the clay, and you are our potter;
  we are all the work of your hand.
Be not exceedingly angry, O LORD,
  and remember not iniquity for ever.

Isaiah 63:16–17,
19—64:7

THESE lines from Isaiah are altogether too much. Any four of them would do. Take the first four. What a question to put to God! We do the wandering, we do the evil—and God gets the blame! And then God gets invited to solve it all as the reading goes on to its "Rend the heavens" lines. Probably everyone has an occasional "Rend the heavens!" day. Some people have "Rend the heavens!" lives. What would that be?

Hunger? Fear? Weakness? Depression? Addiction? Discrimination? How many lives shout to God to tear up the skies and put an end to this unhappiness on the tiny planet Earth! Read Psalm 88 for an extreme example. What reason could anyone have to speak this way to God?

Look at a few December leaves, the old ones blowing around the ground. Isaiah did. What did he see?

"Yet," he says. Yet? Yet, what?

A character in one of J. D. Salinger's short stories says that the most important word in the Bible is "watch." That person would love Advent and especially the gospel: "Be on the watch! Stay awake! Watch with a sharp eye! Look around you! Be on guard!" Why would "watch" be anyone's favorite notion? How do we watch? What are we watching for? Take the question to Isaiah, take it to a saint you have known and one you wish you had known.

What would help us stay awake and watch?   Gabe Huck

O Savior, rend the heavens wide;
Come down, come down with mighty stride;
Unlock the gates, the doors break down;
Unbar the way to heaven's crown.

O Father, light from heaven lend;
As morning dew, O Son, descend.
Drop down, you clouds, the life of spring:
To Jacob's line rain down the King.

O earth, in flow'ring bud be seen;
Clothe hill and dale in garb of green.
Bring forth, O earth, a blossom rare,
Our Savior, sprung from meadow fair.

O Morning Star, O radiant Dawn,
When will we sing your morning song?
Come, Son of God! Without your light
We grope in dread and gloom of night.

Sin's dreadful doom upon us lies;
Grim death looms fierce before our eyes.
Oh, come, lead us with mighty hand
From exile to our promised land.

Friedrich von Spee
Seventeenth century

T HOUGH the Lord has established the signs of the coming,
the time of their fulfillment has not been plainly revealed. These signs have come and gone with a multiplicity
of change; more than that, they are still present. The final
coming is like the first.

Ephrem
Fourth century

R ETURN, O God of love, return,
Earth is a tiresome place;
How long shall we thy children mourn
Our absence from thy face?

Early American
hymn

T HERE were some who spent the savings of several generations on one last spree. Many insulted those they could
not afford to insult and kissed those they shouldn't have
kissed. No one wanted to end up without confession. The
parish priest gave preference to the pregnant and to new
mothers. This self-denying cleric lasted three days and three
nights in the confessional before fainting from an indigestion
of sins.

When midnight came on the last day of the century, all the inhabitants of San Jose de Gracia prepared to die clean. God had accumulated much wrath since the creation of the world, and no one doubted that the time had come for the final blowout. Breath held, eyes closed, teeth clenched, the people listened to the 12 chimes of the church clock, one after the other, deeply convinced that there would be no afterwards.

But there was. For quite awhile now the twentieth century has been on its way; it forges ahead as if nothing had happened. The inhabitants of San Jose de Gracia continue in the same houses, living and surviving among the same mountains of central Mexico—to the disenchantment of the devout who were expecting Paradise, and to the relief of sinners, who find that this little village isn't so bad after all, if one makes comparisons.

Eduardo Galeano

B EHOLD, I am coming soon.

Revelation 22:7

A POCALYPSE is the cry of the helpless, who are borne passively by events which they cannot influence, much less control. The cry of the helpless is often vindictive, expressing impotent rage at reality. Apocalyptic rage is a flight from reality, a plea to God to fulfill their wishes and prove them right and the other wrong. Apocalyptic believers could hardly think the saying, "Go, make disciples of all nations," was addressed to them. Had apocalyptic believers dominated the church since the first century, there would have been no missions to unbelievers, no schools, no hospitals, no orphanages, no almsgiving. The helpless cannot afford to think of such enterprises; they can only await the act of God, and then complain because that act is so long delayed. The gospels and epistles rather tell the believers that they are the act of God.

John L. McKenzie

O N that day they will sing this song
      in the land of Judah:
"A strong city have we;
    [the LORD] sets up walls and ramparts to protect us.
Open up the gates
    to let in a nation that is just,
    one that keeps faith.
A nation of firm purpose you keep in peace;
    in peace, for its trust in you."

Trust in the LORD forever!
    For the LORD is an eternal rock.
[The LORD] humbles those in high places,
    and the lofty city [the LORD] brings down;
[The LORD] tumbles it to the ground,
    levels it with the dust.
It is trampled underfoot by the needy,
    by the footsteps of the poor.

Isaiah 26:1–6

O NE of the distinctive features of this modern anxiety is
      that its victims can never know nightfall. Their whole
lives are spent in the glare of lights, and what bright and
blinding lights they are! These lights are, as it were, the
wayward eyes of our own anxiety, which instinctively try to
shield themselves against God's breakthrough. But they can
glimpse God's coming against the backdrop of darkness,
and therefore they never know rest.

The anxiety-ridden cannot enjoy peace and quiet either.
Their words and actions go on amid the din of unceasing
noise. Their songs and pleasures are loud and slapdash, as if
they were afraid to catch God's alien note in the chorus.
They meticulously drown out silence with incessant talk and
noisy chatter, so that they can stay at peace with themselves.
It is as if stillness were a threatening cloud from which God
might emerge to rend their hearts.

Patience is another quality that the anxiety-ridden cannot display. They cannot patiently cultivate those realities that require slow development and silent blossoming: love and fidelity, mutual understanding and friendship, marriage and family life. That is why these realities are in crisis today to a greater or lesser extent, riddled with an anxiety that cannot stand the slow pace of deliberate, tender care.

Finally, the anxiety-ridden cannot enjoy any peace. From time to time it happens that this anxiety no longer feels able to put up with itself. It seeks to neutralize our imagined alienation in God's advent by arrogantly precipitating our annihilation on its own. It stirs up strife and destruction, it foments war and revolution. The continuing brinkmanship of our age, the powder keg on which we sit, is not a political problem in the last analysis. It is really a religious problem, an outgrowth of our contemporary neurosis and our flight from God's inescapable coming.

The anxiety-ridden secretly hope that their self-instigated destruction will ease the pressure that weighs down upon them. But even our self-wrought destruction passes away, and the anxiety remains. Its mournful cry can be heard amid the debris. It remains because we ourselves remain, because God's advent remains, and because the former cannot fight off the latter.

Johannes Baptist Metz

O ISRAEL, hope in the Lord
both now and forever.

Psalm 131:3

E CCE Rex veniet Dominus terrae,
et ipse auferet jugum captivitatis nostrae.

See! The ruler of the earth shall come,
the Lord who will take from us the heavy burden of our
    exile.

Monastic liturgy

SOON and very soon we are goin' to see the King,
Soon and very soon we are goin' to see the King,
Soon and very soon we are goin' to see the King,
Hallelujah, hallelujah, we're goin' to see the King!

No more cryin' there, we are goin' to see the King,
No more cryin' there, we are goin' to see the King,
No more cryin' there, we are goin' to see the King,
Hallelujah, hallelujah, we're goin' to see the King!

No more dyin' there, we are goin' to see the King,
No more dyin' there, we are goin' to see the King,
No more dyin' there, we are goin' to see the King,
Hallelujah, hallelujah, we're goin' to see the King!

André Couch

DICITE pusillanimes confortamini:
ecce Dominus Deus noster veniet.

Tell the timid to take heart.
The Lord our God will come!

Monastic liturgy

BUT a very little while,
and Lebanon shall be changed into an orchard,
    and the orchard be regarded as a forest!
On that day the deaf shall hear
    the words of a book;
And out of gloom and darkness,
    the eyes of the blind shall see.
The lowly will ever find joy in the LORD,
    and the poor rejoice in the Holy One of Israel.
For the tyrant will be no more
    and the arrogant will have gone;

Therefore thus says the LORD,
  the God of the house of Jacob,
  who redeemed Abraham:
Now Jacob shall have nothing to be ashamed of,
  nor shall his face grow pale.
When his children see
  the work of my hands in his midst,
They shall keep my name holy;
  they shall reverence the Holy One of Jacob,
  and be in awe of the God of Israel.
Those who err in spirit shall acquire understanding,
  and those who find fault shall receive instruction.

Isaiah 29:17–20,
22–24

E XPECTATION—anxious, collective and operative expectation of an end of the world, that is to say, of an issue for
the world—that is perhaps the supreme Christian function
and the most distinctive characteristic of our religion.

Historically speaking, that expectation has never ceased to
guide the progress of our faith like a torch. . . . We persist in
saying that we keep vigil in expectation of the Master. But in
reality we should have to admit, if we were sincere, *that we
no longer expect anything*. The flame must be revived at all
costs. At all costs we must renew in ourselves the desire and
the hope for the great coming. But where are we to look for
the source of this rejuvenation? From the perception of a
more intimate connection between the victory of Christ and
the outcome of the work which our human effort here below
is seeking to construct.

Pierre Teilhard
de Chardin

J UCUNDARE, filia Sion,
exsulta satis filia Jerusalem, alleluia.

Daughter Sion, be glad!
Dance, dance, daughter Jerusalem! Alleluia.

Monastic liturgy

THEY watch for Christ
  who are sensitive, eager, apprehensive in mind,
who are awake, alive, quick-sighted,
    zealous in honoring him,
who look for him in all that happens, and
who would not be surprised,
who would not be over-agitated or overwhelmed,
if they found that he was coming at once. . . .

This then is to watch:
    to be detached from what is present, and
    to live in what is unseen;
    to live in the thought of Christ as he came once,
    and as he will come again;
    to desire his second coming, from our affectionate
    and grateful remembrance of his first.

John Henry Newman
Nineteenth century

MY grief is incurable,
  my heart within me is faint.
Listen! the cry of the daughter of my people,
    far and wide in the land!
Is the LORD no longer in Zion,
    is her King no longer in her midst?
Why do they provoke me with their idols,
    with their foreign nonentities?
"The harvest has passed, the summer is at an end,
    and yet we are not safe!"
I am broken by the ruin of the daughter of my people.
    I am disconsolate; horror has seized me.

Is there no balm in Gilead,
  no physician there?
Why grows not new flesh
  over the wound of the daughter of my people?
Oh, that my head were a spring of water,
  my eyes a fountain of tears,
That I might weep day and night
  over the slain of the daughter of my people!   Jeremiah 8:18–23

WE ask thy grace, O God, that we may make a due use of this holy time. . . . Grant we may be watchful at this time above all others, in avoiding everything that can be injurious to our neighbor, whether in afflicting, or giving scandal, or drawing into sin, or casting any blemish on a reputation; but in all things, O God, may we follow the spirit of charity, being forward in bringing comfort and relief to all, as far as their circumstances shall require, and ours permit.

Grant, O Lord, that thus we may prepare to meet our redeemer.   John Goter

VENIET Dominus et non tardabit,
  ut illuminet abscondita tenebrarum.

The Lord will come soon, will not delay.
The Lord will make the darkest places bright.   Monastic liturgy

WHAT has straw in common with wheat? says the LORD. Is not my word like fire, says the LORD, and like a hammer which breaks the rock in pieces?   Jeremiah 23:29

A voice says: "Cry out!"
I answer, "What shall I cry out?"
"All humankind is grass,
   and all their glory like the flower of the field.
The grass withers, the flower wilts,
   when the breath of the Lord blows upon it.
Though the grass withers and the flower wilts,
Isaiah 40:6−8   the word of our God stands forever."

LEVA Jerusalem oculos, et vide potentiam regis:
ecce Salvator venit solvere te a vinculo.

Lift your eyes, Jerusalem, and see the power of your ruler.
Monastic liturgy   Look to a Savior who shall break your bonds.

MY Lord! what a morning,
my Lord! what a morning,
My Lord! what a morning
when the stars begin to fall.

   You'll hear the trumpet sound
   to wake the nations underground,
   looking to my God's right hand,
   when the stars begin to fall.

   You'll hear the sinner cry
   to wake the nations underground,
   looking to my God's right hand,
   when the stars begin to fall.

   You'll hear the Christian shout
   to wake the nations underground,
Afro-American   looking to my God's right hand,
spiritual   when the stars begin to fall.

Ecce apparebit Dominus, et non mentietur:
si moram fecerit, exspecta eum,
quia veniet, et non tardabit, alleluia.

See! The Lord shall appear, shall not deceive us.
If the Lord tarries, keep watching.
The Lord shall come quickly. Alleluia.   Monastic liturgy

The dominion of heaven shall be compared to ten maidens who took their lamps and went to meet the bridegroom. Five of them were foolish, and five were wise. For when the foolish took their lamps, they took no oil with them; but the wise took flasks of oil with their lamps. As the bridegroom was delayed, they all slumbered and slept. But at midnight there was a cry, "Behold, the bridegroom! Come out to meet him." Then all those maidens rose and trimmed their lamps. And the foolish said to the wise, "Give us some of your oil, for our lamps are going out." But the wise replied, "Perhaps there will not be enough for us and for you; go rather to the dealers and buy for yourselves." And while they went to buy, the bridegroom came, and those who were ready went in with him to the marriage feast; and the door was shut. Afterward the other maidens came also, saying, "Sir, sir, open to us," but he replied, "Truly, I say to you, I do not know you." Watch therefore, for you know neither the day nor the hour.   Matthew 25:1–13

Face to face with our limits,
Blinking before the frightful
Stare of our frailty,
Promise rises
Like a posse of clever maids
Who do not fear the dark
Because their readiness

Lights the search.
Their oil
Becomes the measure of their love,
Their ability to wait—
An indication of their
Capacity to trust and take a chance.
Without the caution or predictability
Of knowing day or hour,
They fall back on that only
Of which they can be sure:
Love precedes them,
Before it
No door will ever close.

T. J. O'Gorman

WHEN the midnight cry began,
Oh, what lamentation,
Thousands sleeping in their sins,
Neglecting their salvation.
Lo, the bridegroom is at hand,
Who will kindly treat him?
Surely all the waiting band
Will now go forth to meet him.

Some, indeed, did wait awhile,
And shone without a rival;
But they spent their seeming oil
Long since the last revival.
Many souls who thought they'd light,
Oh, when the scene was closed,
Now against the Bridegroom fight,
And so they stand opposed.

While the wise are passing by
With all their lamps prepared,

Give us of your oil, they cry,
If any can be spared.
Others trimm'd their former snuff,
Oh, is it not amazing!
Those conclude they've light enough,
And think their lamps are blazing.

Foolish virgins! do you think
Our Bridegroom's a deceiver?
Then may you pass your lives away,
And think to sleep for ever;
But we by faith do see his face,
On whom we have believed;
If there's deception in the case,
'Tis you that are deceived.

Virgins wise, I pray draw near,
And listen to your Savior;
He is your friend, you need not fear,
Oh, why not seek his favor?
He speaks to you in whispers sweet,
In words of consolation:
By grace in him you stand complete,
He is your great salvation.

Dying sinners, will you come,
The Savior now invites you;
His bleeding wounds proclaim there's room
Let nothing then affright you—
Room for you, and room for me,
And room for coming sinners:
Salvation pours a living stream
For you and all believers.

                                        Early American
                                        hymn

HEAR, you maidens, what I shall tell you,
and do at once what I shall command you!
Wait for the bridegroom, Jesus the Savior by name.

Do not fall asleep!
The bridegroom whom you await is here!

He came to earth for your sins,
was born of the virgin in Bethlehem,
was washed and baptized in the Jordan River.

Do not fall asleep!

He was beaten, mocked, abused,
lifted up on the cross and crucified;
he was placed in the tomb.

Do not fall asleep!

And he rose—the scripture tells it!
I am Gabriel, he sent me here,
Wait for him; he shall come soon.

Medieval hymn   Do not fall asleep!

YOU know the time; it is the hour now for you to awake
from sleep. For our salvation is nearer now than when
Romans 13:11–12   we first believed; the night is advanced, the day is at hand.

WAKE, O wake, and sleep no longer,
For he who calls you is no stranger:
Awake, God's own Jerusalem!
Hear, the midnight bells are chiming
The signal for his royal coming:
Let voice to voice announce his name!
We feel his footsteps near,

The Bridegroom at the door—
Alleluia!
The lamps will shine
With light divine
As Christ the savior comes to reign.

Zion hears the sound of singing;
Our hearts are thrilled with sudden longing:
She stirs, and wakes, and stands prepared.
Christ, her friend and lord and lover,
Her star and sun and strong redeemer—
At last his mighty voice is heard.
The Son of God has come
To make with us his home:
Sing Hosanna!
The fight is won,
The feast begun:
We fix our eyes on Christ alone.

Glory, glory, sing the angels,
While music sounds from strings and cymbals;
All humankind, with songs arise!
Twelve the gates into the city,
Each one a pearl of shining beauty;
The streets of gold ring out with praise.
All creatures round the throne
Adore the holy One
With rejoicing:
Amen be sung
By ev'ry tongue
To crown their welcome to the King.

Philipp Nicolai
Sixteenth century

Shaker song
Nineteenth century

Awake, my soul, arise and shake,
  No time to ever ponder,
Keep awake, keep awake
  Lest ye be rent asunder.
I will be good, I will be free,
  I'll hate the old deceiver.
No earthly tie shall fetter me,
  I'll be a good believer.

Night is drawing nigh—" How long the road is. But, for all the time the journey has already taken, how you have needed every second of it in order to learn what the road passes-by.

Dag Hammarskjöld

Why are you standing there looking up at the sky? This Jesus who has been taken up from you into heaven will return in the same way as you have seen him going into heaven.

Acts 1:11

Whatever was written previously was written for our instruction, that by endurance and by the encouragement of the scriptures we might have hope. May the God of endurance and encouragement grant us to think in harmony with one another, in keeping with Christ Jesus, that with one accord you may with one voice glorify the God and Father of our Lord Jesus Christ. May the God of hope fill you with all joy and peace in believing, so that you may abound in hope by the power of the Holy Spirit.

Romans 15:4–6, 13

JERUSALEM gaude gaudio magno,
quia veniet tibi salvator, alleluia.

Rejoice, Jerusalem, with the greatest joy:
The savior will come to you. Alleluia.   Monastic liturgy

BLOW the trumpet in Zion,
sound the alarm on my holy mountain!
Let all who dwell in the land tremble,
    for the day of the LORD is coming.   Joel 2:1

THUS the word of the Lord came to me: Son of man, speak
this prophecy: Thus says the Lord GOD: Cry, Oh, the
day! for near is the day, near is the day of the LORD; a day of
clouds, doomsday for the nations shall it be.   Ezekiel 30:1–3

GATHER, gather yourselves together,
O nation without shame!
Before you are driven away,
    like chaff that passes on;
Before there comes upon you
    the blazing anger of the LORD;
Before there comes upon you
    the day of the LORD's anger.
Seek justice, seek humility;
    perhaps you may be sheltered
    on the day of the LORD's anger.   Zephaniah 2:1–3

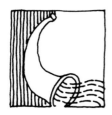

MICHAEL haul your boat ashore, alleluia.
Then you'll hear the horn they blow, alleluia.

Then you'll hear the trumpet sound, alleluia.
Trumpet sound the world around, alleluia.

Trumpet sound the jubilee, alleluia.
Trumpet sound for you and me, alleluia.

Trumpet sound for rich and poor, alleluia.
Michael haul your boat ashore, alleluia.

Afro-American
spiritual

WOE to those who yearn for the day of the LORD!
What will this day of the LORD mean for you?
Darkness, and not light!

Amos 5:18

ABOVE the clamor of our violence
your word of truth resounds,
O God of majesty and power.
Over nations enshrouded in despair
your justice dawns.
Grant your household
a discerning spirit and a watchful eye
to perceive the hour in which we live.
Hasten the advent of that day
when the weapons of war shall be banished,
our deeds of darkness cast off,
and all your scattered children gathered into one.
We ask this through him whose coming is certain,
whose day draws near:
your Son, our Lord Jesus Christ,
who lives and reigns with you and the Holy Spirit,
one God, for ever and ever.

Prayer,
First Sunday of Advent

THIS old night, this old night,
   Every night and all,
Fire, and sleet, and candle light,
   And Christ receive thy soul.   A lyke-wake dirge

ALONE, alone, about a dreadful wood
   Of conscious evil runs a lost mankind,
Dreading to find its Father lest it find
The Goodness it has dreaded is not good:
Alone, alone, about our dreadful wood.

Where is that Law for which we broke our own,
Where now that Justice for which Flesh resigned
Her hereditary right to passion, Mind
His will to absolute power? Gone. Gone.
Where is that Law for which we broke our own?

The Pilgrim Way has led to the Abyss.
Was it to meet such grinning evidence
We left our richly odoured ignorance?
Was the triumphant answer to be this?
The Pilgrim Way has led to the Abyss.

We who must die demand a miracle.
How could the Eternal do a temporal act,
The Infinite become a finite fact?
Nothing can save us that is possible:
We who must die demand a miracle.   W. H. Auden

SOMETIMES I feel like a motherless child,
   Sometimes I feel like a motherless child,
Sometimes I feel like a motherless child,
                                                     Afro-American
A long way from home, a long way from home.   spiritual

W E are a wounded people;
we can love each other, forgive each other
and celebrate together our oneness.
Perhaps we can only truly accept this humiliation
if we live an experience similar to the one
lived by the prodigal son.
If we discover that we are loved and forgiven
   and accepted by the Father just as we are,
   in all our brokenness,
   with all the darkness and pain inside us,
then we too can weep in the arms of God,
rejoicing in his forgiveness.

Yes the cry and the anguish of the poor
triggers off our own cry and anguish;
we touch our point of pain and helplessness.

But then we discover the new name of God,
the name revealed by Jesus,
of the Spirit, the Holy Spirit;
the Father will send a "Paraclete."
It is a beautiful name, meaning literally
"the one who answers the cry or the call,"
like a mother
who takes in her arms her weeping child.
She is a paraclete.
The name of God is "the one who answers the cry."
Mercy and misery embrace!
We can only know the incredible mercy and love of God
if we accept to descend into our misery
and there cry out to him.
Then he will answer, "Here I am, Beloved,"
and will enfold us in his arms

Jean Vanier   with a long embrace.

O SHEPHERD of Israel, hear us,
you who lead Jacob's flock,
shine forth from your cherubim throne
upon Ephraim, Benjamin, Manasseh.

O Lord, raise up your might,
O Lord, come to our help.
God of hosts, bring us back;
let your face shine on us and we shall be saved.   Psalm 80:2–4

S AINT Nicholas. *Day of death:* (according to the mar-
tyrology) December 6, about 360. *Grave:* originally at
Myra; since 1087 at Bari in Italy. *Life* (highly legendary):
Nicholas was born at Patara in Asia Minor to parents who,
having long been childless, had petitioned God with many
prayers. Already as a youth Nicholas became noted for his
zeal in helping the unfortunate and oppressed. In his native
city there lived a poor nobleman who had three marriage-
able daughters; he could not obtain a suitor for them
because he could offer no dowry. The contemptible idea
struck him to sacrifice the innocence of his daughters to gain
the needed money. When Nicholas became aware of this,
he went by night and threw a bag containing as much gold as
was needed for a dowry through the window. This he
repeated the second and third nights. During a sea voyage
he calmed the storm by his prayer; he is therefore venerated
as patron of sailors. On a certain occasion he was
imprisoned for the faith. In a wonderful way he later became
bishop of Myra; his presence is noted at the Council of
Nicaea. He died a quiet death in his episcopal city, uttering
the words: "Into your hands I commend my spirit."

Nicholas is highly venerated in the East as a miracle worker,
as "preacher of the word of God, spokesman of the Father."   Pius Parsch

THE celebration of the feast of the nativity of Christ in the Orthodox church is patterned after the celebration of the feast of the Lord's resurrection. A fast of forty days precedes the feast, with special preparatory days announcing the approaching birth of the Savior. Thus, on St. Andrew's Day (November 30) and St. Nicholas Day (December 6) songs are sung to announce the coming birthday of the Lord.

Adorn yourself, O cavern.
Make yourself ready, O manger.
O shepherds and magi,
    bring your gifts and bear witness.
For the Virgin is coming
    bearing Christ in her womb.

Thomas Hopko

O you who love festivals,
    Come gather and sing the praises
    of the fair beauty of bishops,
The glory of the fathers,
The fountain of wonders and great protector
    of the faithful.

Let us all say: Rejoice, O guardian of the people of Myra,
Their head and honored counsellor,
The pillar of the church which cannot be shaken.

Rejoice, O light full of brightness
That makes the ends of the world shine with wonders.

Rejoice, O divine delight of the afflicted,
The fervent advocate of those who suffer from injustice.

And now, O all-blessed Nicholas,
Never cease praying to Christ our God
For those who honor the festival of your memory
With faith and with love.

Orthodox liturgy

W HAT keeps you from giving now? Isn't the poor person there? Aren't your own warehouses full? Isn't the reward promised? The command is clear: the hungry person is dying now, the naked person is freezing now, the person in debt is beaten now—and you want to wait until tomorrow? "I'm not doing any harm," you say. "I just want to keep what I own, that's all." You own! You are like someone who sits down in a theater and keeps everyone else away, saying that what is there for everyone's use is your own. . . . If everyone took only what they needed and gave the rest to those in need, there would be no such thing as rich and poor. After all, didn't you come into life naked, and won't you return naked to the earth?

The bread in your cupboard belongs to the hungry person; the coat hanging unused in your closet belongs to the person who needs it; the shoes rotting in your closet belong to the person with no shoes; the money which you put in the bank belongs to the poor. You do wrong to everyone you could help, but fail to help.

Basil
Fourth century

T HE large rooms of which you are so proud are in fact your shame. They are big enough to hold crowds—and also big enough to shut out the voice of the poor. . . . There is your sister or brother, naked, crying! And you stand confused over the choice of an attractive floor covering.

Ambrose
Fourth century

A voyce from heven to erth shal com:
"Venite ad iudicium."

This voyce both sharp and also shryll
Shal be herd from heven to hell;
All mydle erthe it shall fulfyll:
  "Venite ad iudicium."

"Venite" is a blyssed song
For them that for joye dooth longe
And shall forsake paynes strong:
    "Venite ad iudicium."

Glad in hert may they be
Whan Chryst sayeth, "Venite;
Ye blyssed chyldren, come to me,
    Into vitam eternam.

"Whan I hongred, ye gave me meat;
Ye clothed me agaynst the heat;
In trouble ye dyde me not forget;
    Venite ad iudicium.

"Ye socoured me at your doore
And for my sake gave to the poore;
Therfore wyll I you socoure;
    Venite ad iudicium."

Sory in hert may they be
That hereth this hevy worde: "Ite;
Ye cursed chyldren, go fro me,
    Into ignem eternum.

"Whan for nede that I dyde crye,
Comfortlesse ye lete me dye;
Therfore now I you deny;
    Venite ad iudicium.

"For by me ye set no store,
Ye shall abye ryght dere therfore
In hell with devyls for evermore;
    Venite ad iudicium."

English carol
Sixteenth century

CHILDREN'S Letters: This is an ancient Advent custom, widespread in Europe, Canada and South America. When children go to bed on the eve of St. Nicholas Day, they put upon the windowsills little notes which they have written or dictated, addressed to the Child Jesus. These letters, containing lists of desired Christmas presents, are supposed to be taken to heaven by St. Nicholas or by angels. In South America the children write their notes to the "little Jesus" during the days from December 16 to 24 and put them in front of the crib, whence, they believe, angels take them to heaven during the night.

Francis X. Weiser

A desire to be truthful with our children has made many people uncomfortable with one of the few myths retained in our cultic celebrations at Christmastime, the concept of Santa Claus or St. Nicholas. On the one hand we know in our very bones the power and magic of this figure— or certainly he would not be such a persistent force in this season—but on the other hand we don't know how long we can or should allow children to believe in him or what it is that they should believe.

I don't want to get rid of Santa Claus. But I think that we need to give our Santa Claus, who has evolved out of a very ancient St. Nicholas, a closer examination. A myth is an exceptionally difficult thing to kill, for it continues to be devastatingly revealing even when we have tampered with it and changed its form by our rationalizations or our moralistic applications. A figure who can endure with such tenacity ever since the fourth century, and with a stunning continuity of legends and similarity of iconographic representations in so many countries, has got to be real. He may well be the most popular saint the world has ever known, whether he was ever real in history or not. His legends cannot be brushed aside as "mere" myths because they live on into the present and refuse to die while stories in history, on the other hand, deal with what is dead and past. Santa Claus is the father figure we all dream about and share in our collective unconscious. He is a type of God the Father, primal and powerful and, yes, real.

Gertrud Mueller Nelson

OUR eyes are blinded by the holiness you bear.
The bishop's robe, the mitre and the cross of gold
Obscure the simple man within the saint.
Strip off your glory, Nicolas, and speak!

Across the tremendous bridge of sixteen-hundred years
I come to stand in worship with you
As I stood among my faithful congregation long ago.
All who knelt beside me then are gone.
Their name is dust, their tombs are grass and clay,
Yet still their shining seed of faith survives
    In you!
It weathers time, it springs again
    In you!
With you it stands like forest oak
Or withers with the grasses underfoot.
Preserve the living faith for which your ancestors fought!
For faith was won by centuries of sacrifice
And many martyrs died
That you might worship God.

Help us, Lord! to find the hidden road
That leads from love to greater Love, from faith
To greater Faith.
    Strengthen us, O Lord!
Eric Crozier   Screw up our strength to serve thee with simplicity.

THERE shall come forth a shoot from the stump of Jesse,
and a branch shall grow out of its roots.
Upon this one the Spirit of the LORD shall rest,
the spirit of wisdom and understanding,
the spirit of counsel and might,
the spirit of knowledge and the fear of the LORD.
And his delight shall be in the fear of the LORD.
He shall not judge by what the eyes see,
or decide by what the ears hear;
but with righteousness he shall judge the poor,
and decide with equity for the meek of the earth;
and he shall smite the earth with the rod of his mouth,
and with the breath of his lips shall slay the wicked.
Righteousness shall be the belt of his waist,
and faithfulness shall gird his loins.
The wolf shall dwell with the lamb,
and the leopard shall lie down with the kid,
and the calf and the lion and the fatling together,
and a little child shall lead them.
The cow and the bear shall feed;
their young shall lie down together;
and the lion shall eat straw like the ox.
The sucking child shall play over the hole of the asp,
and the weaned child shall put a hand on the adder's den.
They shall not hurt or destroy
in all my holy mountain;
for the earth shall be full of the knowledge of the LORD
as the waters cover the sea.

In that day there will stand as an ensign to the peoples the
root of Jesse, whom the nations shall seek, and whose
dwellings shall be glorious.   Isaiah 11:1–10

W E'RE gonna sit at the welcome table!
We're gonna sit at the welcome table
one of these days! Hallelujah!
We're gonna sit at the welcome table!
Gonna sit at the welcome table one of these days.

All kinds of people around that table
one of these days! Hallelujah!
All kinds of people round that table!
Gonna sit at the welcome table one of these days.

Afro-American spiritual

C ONVERTERE Domine aliquantulum,
et ne tardes venire ad servos tuos.

Turn toward us, Lord, if only for a moment.
Hurry to your servants!

Monastic liturgy

O Adam and Eve, lay aside your sorrow.
Behold, a barren womb today
wondrously bears fruit:
The mother of our Joy!

O father Abraham and all the patriarchs,
Rejoice greatly, seeing your seed blossom:
The mother of our God!

Rejoice, O Anna! Joachim, rejoice!
Today in wondrous manner you bear to the world
The fruit of grace and salvation!

O choir of prophets, rejoice exceedingly!
For behold, today Anna bears the holy fruit
You foretold to us.

Rejoice, all nations!
The barren Anna conceives the fruit of her womb;
By persevering in hope, she bears our life!

Rejoice, O ends of the earth!
Behold the barren mother conceives her
Who without human seed will bear the creator of all!

Today a royal robe of purple and fine linen
Is woven from the loins of David.
The mystical flower of Jesse is blossoming
From which comes Christ our God,
        the savior of our souls.   Orthodox liturgy

THIS is the truth sent from above,
The truth of God, the God of love,
Therefore don't turn me from your door,
But harken all both rich and poor.

The first thing which I do relate
Is that God did man create;
The next thing which to you I'll tell—
Woman was made with man to dwell.

Then after this was God's own choice
To place them both in Paradise,
There to remain from evil free
Except if they ate from such a tree.

And they did eat, which was a sin,
And thus their ruin did begin;
Ruined themselves, both you and me
And all of our posterity.

Thus we were heirs to endless woes,
Till God the Lord did interpose;
And so a promise soon did run
That he would redeem us by his Son.   English carol

THE man and the woman heard the sound of the LORD God walking in the garden in the cool of the day, and they hid themselves from the presence of the LORD God among the trees of the garden. But the LORD God called to the man, and said to him, "Where are you?" And he said, "I heard the sound of you in the garden, and I was afraid, because I was naked; and I hid myself." God said, "Who told you that you were naked? Have you eaten of the tree of which I commanded you not to eat?" The man said, "The woman whom you gave to be with me, she gave me fruit of the tree, and I ate." Then the LORD God said to the woman, "What is this that you have done?" The woman said, "The serpent beguiled me, and I ate." The LORD God said to the serpent,

"Because you have done this,
     cursed are you above all cattle,
     and above all wild animals;
upon your belly you shall go,
     and dust you shall eat
     all the days of your life.
I will put enmity between you and the woman,
     and between your offspring and her offspring;
her offspring shall bruise your head,
     and you shall bruise his heel."
To the woman God said,
     "I will greatly multiply your pain in childbearing;
     in pain you shall bring forth children,
yet your desire shall be for your husband,
     and he shall rule over you."

And to Adam God said,

"Because you have listened to the voice of your wife,
     and have eaten of the tree
of which I commanded you,
     'You shall not eat of it,'
cursed is the ground because of you;
     in toil you shall eat of it all the days of your life;
thorns and thistles it shall bring forth to you;

and you shall eat the plants of the field.
In the sweat of your face
   you shall eat bread
till you return to the ground,
   for out of it you were taken;
you are dust,
   and to dust you shall return."

The man called his wife's name Eve, because she was the mother of all living. And the LORD God made for Adam and for his wife garments of skins, and clothed them.   Genesis 3:8–21

N E timeas Maria.
   Do not be afraid, Mary.   Monastic Liturgy

T HE Theotokos has been revealed on the earth in truth,
   Proclaimed of old by the words of the prophets,
Foretold by the wise patriarchs
   and the company of the righteous.
She will exchange glad tidings with the honor of women:
Sarah, Rebecca, and glorious Hannah,
And Miriam, the sister of Moses.
All the ends of the earth shall rejoice with them,
Together with all of creation.
For God shall come to be born in the flesh,
Granting the world great mercy.   Orthodox liturgy

THAT man say we can't have as much rights as a man 'cause Christ wasn't a woman. Where did your Christ come from? From God and a woman. Man had nothing to do with it.

Sojourner Truth
Nineteenth century

OF man's first disobedience, and the fruit
Of that forbidden tree whose mortal taste
With loss of Eden, till one greater Man
Restore us, and regain the blissful seat,
Sing, Heavenly Muse, that, on the secret top
Of Oreb, or Sinai, didst inspire
That shepherd who first taught the chosen seed
In the beginning how the Heavens and Earth
Rose out of Chaos: or, if Sion hill
Delight thee more, and Siloa's brook that flowed
Fast by the oracle of God, I thence
Invoke thy aid to my adventurous song,
That with no middle flight intends to soar
Above th' Aonian mount, while it pursues
Things unattempted yet in prose or rhyme.
And chiefly thou, O Spirit, that dost prefer
Before all temples th' upright heart and pure,
Instruct me, for thou know'st; thou from the first
Wast present, and, with mighty wings outspread,
Dovelike sat'st brooding on the vast abyss,
And mad'st it pregnant: What is in me dark,
Illumine; what is low, raise and support;
That, to the height of this great argument,
I may assert Eternal Providence,
And justify the ways of God to men.

John Milton
Seventeenth century

V IRTUS Altissimi obumbrabit tibi.
The power of the Most High will overshadow you.   Monastic liturgy

H AIL Mary, the most beautiful dove, which carried the word of God for us; we greet you with the Archangel Gabriel saying: Hail Mary, full of grace, the Lord is with you. Hail, O Virgin, the glory of our race; you have borne Emmanuel for us. We pray that you will remember us before the Lord Jesus Christ, that he will forgive us our sins.   Coptic liturgy

H AIL, O most worthy in all the world!
Thou purest Maiden that ever on earth
Through the long ages lived among humankind!
Rightly all mortals in blithe mood
Name thee blessed and hail thee bride
Of the king of glory. The thanes of Christ,
In heaven the highest, carol and sing
Proclaiming thee lady of the heavenly legions,
Of earthly orders, and the hosts of hell.

Thou bring thy maidenhood unto thy maker,
Presenting it there unspotted of sin.
Of all humankind there came no other,
No bride with linked jewels, like unto thee
With pure heart sending thy glorious gift
To its heavenly home. The Lord of triumph
Sent forth his herald from the hosts on high
To bring thee knowledge of abundant grace:
That in pure birth thou should'st bear God's Son
In mercy to people; and thou thyself, Mary,
Remain for ever immaculate maid.   English lyric

O God, you are my God, for you I long;
  for you my soul is thirsting.
My body pines for you
like a dry, weary land without water.
So I gaze on you in the sanctuary
to see your strength and your glory.

For your love is better than life,
my lips will speak your praise.
So I will bless you all my life,
in your name I will lift up my hands.
My soul shall be filled as with a banquet,
my mouth shall praise you with joy.

On my bed I remember you.
On you I muse through the night
for you have been my help;
in the shadow of your wings I rejoice.
My soul clings to you;
Psalm 63:2–9   your right hand holds me fast.

A SK not, doubt not. You have, my heart, already chosen
  the joy of Advent. As a force against your own uncer-
tainty, bravely tell yourself, "It is the Advent of the great
God." Say this with faith and love, and then both the past of
your life, which has become holy, and your life's eternal,
boundless future will draw together in the now of this world.
For then into the heart comes the one who is Advent, the
boundless future who is already in the process of coming,
the Lord, who has already come into the time of the flesh to
Karl Rahner   redeem it.

I don't know what will happen now. We've got some difficult days ahead. But it really doesn't matter with me now, because I've been to the mountaintop. And I don't mind. Like anybody, I would like to have a long life; longevity has its place. But I'm not concerned about that now. I just want to do God's will. And he's allowed me to go up to the mountain. And I've looked over. And I've seen the promised land. I may not get there with you. But I want you to know tonight that we as a people will get to the promised land. And I'm happy tonight, I'm not worried about anything. I'm not fearing any man. Mine eyes have seen the glory of the coming of the Lord.

Martin Luther King, Jr.

AT the coming of the Most High our hearts shall be made clean, and we shall walk worthily in the way of the Lord. The Lord is coming and will not delay.

Cistercian liturgy

DA mercedem, Domine, sustinentibus te,
ut prophetae tui fideles inveniantur.

Have mercy on those who wait for you, Lord,
and you shall find your prophets keeping faith.

Monastic liturgy

THE Advent mystery is the beginning of the end of all in us that is not yet Christ.

Thomas Merton

MERTON'S most important experience in his whole Asian trip came at Polonnaruwa. He went to visit the giant Buddhas and took a series of superb photographs of them.

I am able to approach the Buddhas barefoot and undisturbed, my feet in wet grass, wet sand. The silence of the extraordinary faces. The great smiles. Huge and yet subtle. Filled with every possibility, questioning nothing, knowing everything, rejecting nothing, the peace not of emotional refutation . . . that has seen through every question without trying to discredit anyone or anything—*without refutation*—without establishing some other argument. For the doctrinaire, the mind that needs well-established positions, such peace, such silence, can be frightening. I was knocked over with a rush of relief and thankfulness at the *obvious* clarity of the figures. . . . Looking at these figures I was suddenly, almost forcibly, jerked clean out of the habitual, half-tied vision of things, and an inner clearness, clarity, as if exploding from the rocks themselves, became evident and obvious. . . . I don't know when in my life I have ever had such a sense of beauty and spiritual validity running together in one aesthetic illumination. Surely, with Mahabalipuram and Polonnaruwa my Asian pilgrimage has come clear and purified itself. I mean, I know and have seen what I was obscurely looking for. I don't know what else remains but I have now seen and have pierced through the surface and have got beyond the shadow and the disguise.

That was on December 4. . . . [On December 10, after addressing the conference in Bangkok,] Merton had lunch and did disappear to his room, commenting to a colleague on the way about how much he was looking forward to having a siesta. In a long letter later written by the delegates at the Conference to Dom Flavian what then occurred was expressed in the following words: "Not long after he retired a shout was heard by others in his cottage, but after a preliminary check they thought they must have imagined the cry.

"He was found at the end of the meridian (afternoon rest) and when found was lying on the floor. He was on his back with the electric fan lying across his chest. The fan was still switched on, and there was a deep burn and some cuts on his right side and arm. The back of his head was also bleeding slightly."

Perhaps any death brings with it both a sense of surprise and a sense of its inevitability. There are always those, and there were many after Merton's death, who feel that it somehow "had to be like that." Merton had, from time to time, both spoken and written comments that suggested that his death might come early. Some of his friends commented on the extraordinary, almost Zen-like way that death had come to him. Fewer people than one might expect noted that he died on the same day as the great Protestant theologian Karl Barth, and it was a measure of the ecumenism in Louisville, which Merton had been instrumental in promoting, that Catholics and Protestants there united in a joint memorial service for both of them.

Many years before Naomi Burton had made the suggestion, humorously, that Merton was accident-prone. "I couldn't help noticing that it's your visitors who get locked out of the church, and your server who forgets things, and your vestments that get caught in the folding chair. . . . I find your incredible adventures with nature and with publishing extremely endearing." Perhaps Merton was accident-prone; perhaps, like many intellectuals, he tended to get lost in his thinking, and absentmindedly forgot about the dangers of touching electrical equipment with wet hands; perhaps the fan was merely faulty. Perhaps, however, he had finished his life six days before at Polonnaruwa and was called to the God he had loved and served so well.

Monica Furlong

T HE sermon I gave [at the conference on monasticism on the morning after Merton's death] was a moment of talking about Merton's search for God. When a monk enters a monastery, what is asked of him is "Are you truly seeking

God?" The question isn't "Have you found God?" The question is "Is he seeking God? Is his motivation highly involved in that search of who and what God is in relationship to us?" It's not philosophical—it's existential. And Merton, to me, was a great searcher. He was constantly unhappy, as all great searchers are. He was constantly ill at ease, he was constantly restless, as all searchers are— because that's part of the search. And in that sense he was the perfect monk. Contemplation isn't satisfaction—it's search.

Rembert Weakland

A LL of the branches
None of the roots.
All of the words—
Freedom branches
All of the words
Happiness branches
All of the words
Equality branches
None of the roots.
All of the branches
None of the roots.

Thomas Merton

C HARM with your stainlessness these winter nights,
Skies, and be perfect!
Fly vivider in the fiery dark, you quiet meteors,
And disappear.
You moon, be slow to go down,
This is your fill!

The four white roads make off in silence
Towards the four parts of the starry universe.
Time falls like manna at the corners of the wintry earth.
We have become more humble than the rocks,
More wakeful than the patient hills.

Charm with your stainlessness these nights in Advent,
    holy spheres,
While minds, as meek as beasts,
Stay close at home in the sweet hay;
And intellects are quieter than the flocks that feed
    by starlight.

Oh pour your darkness and your brightness over all our
    solemn valleys,
Your skies: and travel like the gentle Virgin,
Towards the planets' stately setting,

Oh white full moon as quiet as Bethlehem!   Thomas Merton

PEACE is more than the absence of war: it cannot be reduced to the maintenance of a balance of power between opposing forces nor does it arise out of despotic dominion, but it is appropriately called "the effect of righteousness" (Isaiah 32:17). It is the fruit of that right ordering of things with which the divine founder has invested human society and which must be actualized by humans thirsting after an ever more perfect reign of justice. . . .

Peace cannot be obtained on earth unless human welfare is safeguarded and people freely and trustingly share with one another the riches of their minds and their talents. A firm determination to respect the dignity of others and other peoples along with the deliberate practice of love are absolutely necessary for the achievement of peace. Accordingly, peace is also the fruit of love, for love goes beyond what justice can ensure. . . .

Therefore, all Christians are earnestly to speak the truth in love (cf. Ephesians 4:15) and join with all who love peace in pleading for peace and trying to bring it about. In the same spirit we cannot but express our admiration for all who forgo the use of violence to vindicate their rights and resort to those other means of defense which are available to weaker parties, provided it can be done without harm to the rights and duties of others and of the community.

Insofar as all are sinners, the threat of war hangs over them and will so continue until the coming of Christ; but insofar as they can vanquish sin by coming together in charity, violence itself will be vanquished and they will make these words come true: "They shall beat their swords into plowshares, and their spears into pruning hooks; nation shall not lift up sword against nation, neither shall they learn war any more" (Isaiah 2:4).

Vatican II
The Church in the
Modern World

I 'M gonna lay down my sword and shield
Down by the riverside, down by the riverside,
   down by the riverside.
I'm gonna lay down my sword and shield
Down by the riverside, down by the riverside!

I ain't gonna study war no more!
I ain't gonna study war no more!
I ain't gonna study war no more!
I ain't gonna study war no more!
I ain't gonna study war no more!
I ain't gonna study war no more!

Afro-American
spiritual

T AKE off the garment of your sorrow and affliction,
O Jerusalem,
   and put on for ever the beauty of the glory from God.
Put on the robe of the righteousness from God;

put on your head the diadem of the glory of
    the Everlasting.
For God will show your splendor everywhere
    under heaven.
For your name will for ever be called by God,
    "Peace of righteousness and glory of godliness."
Arise, O Jerusalem, stand upon the height
    and look toward the east,
and see your children gathered from west to east,
    at the word of the Holy One,
    rejoicing that God has remembered them.
For they went forth from you on foot,
    led away by their enemies;
but God will bring them back to you,
    carried in glory, as on a royal throne.
For God has ordered that every high mountain and the
    everlasting hills be made low
    and the valleys filled up, to make level ground,
    so that Israel may walk safely in the glory of God.
The woods and every fragrant tree
    have shaded Israel at God's command.
For God will lead Israel with joy,
    in the light of the divine glory,
    with the mercy and righteousness that come from God.   Baruch 5:1–9

F ATHER in heaven,
  the day draws near when the glory of your Son
will make radiant the night of the waiting world.
May the lure of greed not impede us from the joy
which moves the hearts of those who seek him.
May the darkness not blind us to the visions of wisdom
which fills the minds of those who find him.   Roman rite

Peter Chrysologus
Fifth century

G OD saw the world falling to ruin because of fear and immediately acted to call it back with love. God invited it by grace, preserved it by love, and embraced it with compassion.

Vatican II
The Church in the
Modern World

T HE joy and hope, the grief and anguish of the people of our time, especially of those who are poor or afflicted in any way, are the joy and hope, the grief and anguish of the followers of Christ as well. Nothing that is genuinely human fails to find an echo in their hearts. For theirs is a community composed of human beings who, united in Christ and guided by the Holy Spirit, press onwards towards the kingdom of the Father and are bearers of a message of salvation intended for all. That is why Christians cherish a feeling of deep solidarity with the human race and its history.

W HERE are you going?" asks Mary of Juan Diego. He is stopped in his tracks. He leaves his "important" plans and becomes her messenger: Build a church where the cries of the poor and the oppressed will be heard. The bishop hears these gospel-laden words with shock and disbelief. Signs, tangible signs, to know if this is true: That is his demand. But the words that the Indian brings are the answer. The church must turn its institutional attention from its needs to listen to the solitary voice of one poor man. It is a voice caught up in cultural traditions, old Indian ways, unpurified beliefs. Juan Diego's nervous intensity comes not from self-interest but from the faith that his voice and prayer have been heard by God. The words he speaks are the answer to his prayers.

What Mary has asked of the bishop is not meant to cause a division among the servants of the Lord. It is not a condemnation of strategies or theologies. Rather, it is a word of direction to move from the status quo operations of the day and to build up a place where the prayers, the cries, the heartbreak of people can be heard. The place becomes symbolic of the fact that a mestizo church emerges from these birth sufferings of a conquered people. The temple is symbolic of the age-old, faithful word of God: to be with the people.

Guadalupe's significance is both word and symbol. She provides the answers to the prayers of her faithful people: "God is with you!" Her very appearance, as one of the poor, aligns her with them. Guadalupe's proclamation can be seen as God's option for the poor.

"Where are you going?" echoes in the life of God's poor to this present day.   Arturo Pérez

THEY'VE come to sing in your honor
    from the desert and the forest,
From valleys deep in the mountains;
    they make a joyful chorus.
They've brought their drums and their dances,
    ancient ways their parents taught them;
Their village saints and their banners,
    ev'ry group made sure they brought them.

    O Mother dark and lovely,
        hear the poor who come with their song;
    Lead them into Jesus' kingdom
        where they truly do belong.

From Vera Cruz and Nogales,
    from old Taxco with its fountains,
Tehuantepec, Zacatecas,
    and Durango in the mountains;
They come from humid Tampico,
    Matamoros near the river,

From ranchos deep in Sonora
  where the cottonwoods still quiver.

They dance to show they love you,
  out of faith and deep emotion,
They offer flowers and candles
  as a sign of their devotion.
The children run and are laughing
  all are sure that you still love them,
While parents weep out of gladness,
Willard F. Jabusch   for your picture's there above them.

I N an age which offers a variety of escapes from the human
condition, Christians are more than ever a sign of contradiction. They continue to believe that the search for God
must begin with the acceptance of the human. They believe
this because it is in the stable of humanity that God has come
in search of us.

In the human experience of Jesus, God became available to
us as the depth of human life. Thus, a Christian believes that
the experience of ultimate meaning comes not from a leap
out of the human condition, but a journey through its dark
John Heagle   waters.

W ITH the drawing of this Love and the voice
of this Calling

We shall not cease from exploration
And the end of all our exploring
Will be to arrive where we started
T. S. Eliot   And know the place for the first time.

R ISE up, Lord, in defense of your people,
do not hide your face from our troubles.
Father of orphans,
wealth of the poor,
we rejoice in making you known;
may we find comfort and security
in times of pain and anxiety.

Liturgy of the Hours

D ELIVER us, O Lord, from our bondage
as streams in dry land.
Those who are sowing in tears
will sing when they reap.

Psalm 126:4–5

T HE Uruguayan political prisoners may not talk without
permission, or whistle, smile, sing, walk fast, or greet
other prisoners; nor may they make or receive drawings of
pregnant women, couples, butterflies, stars or birds.

One Sunday, Didasko Pérez, school teacher, tortured and
jailed "for having ideological ideas," is visited by his daughter Milay, aged five. She brings him a drawing of birds. The
guards destroy it at the entrance of the jail.

On the following Sunday, Milay brings him a drawing of
trees. Trees are not forbidden, and the drawings get through.
Didasko praises her work and asks about the colored circles
scattered in the treetops, many small circles half-hidden
among the branches: "Are they oranges? What fruit is it?"
The child puts her finger to her mouth: "Sssssshhh."

And she whispers in his ear: "Silly. Don't you see they're
eyes? They're the eyes of the birds that I've smuggled in for
you."

Eduardo Galeano

LUCY died during the persecutions of Diocletian at Catania in Sicily, being beheaded by the sword. Her body was later brought to Constantinople and finally Venice, where she is now resting in the church of Santa Lucia.

Because her name means "light," she very early became the great patron saint for the "light of the body"—the eyes. All over Christianity her help was invoked against diseases of the eyes, especially the danger of blindness. The lighters of street lamps in past centuries had her as patron saint and made a special ceremony of their task on the eve of December 13.

Saint Lucy attained immense popularity in medieval times because, before the calendar reform, her feast happened to fall on the shortest day of the year. Again because of her name, many of the ancient light and fire customs of the Yuletide became associated with her day. Thus we find "Lucy candles" lighted in homes and "Lucy fires" burned in the open. In Scandinavia before the Reformation, Saint Lucy Day was one of unusual celebration and festivity because, for the people of Sweden and Norway, she was the great "light saint" who turned the tides of their long winter and brought the light of day to renewed victory.

A popular custom in Scandinavia on the eve of December 13 is for children to write the word "Lussi" on doors, fences and walls. With the word always goes the picture of a female figure (Saint Lucy). The purpose of this practice in ancient times was to announce to the demons of winter that their reign was broken on Saint Lucy's Day, that the sun would return again and the days become longer.

"Lucy fires" used to be burned everywhere in northern Europe on December 13. Into these bonfires people threw incense and, while the flames rose, trumpets and flutes played to greet the changing of the sun's course. These fires were greatly valued as a powerful protection against disease, witchcraft and dangers, and people would stand nearby and let the smoke of the incense reach them, thus obtaining the desired "protection."

Francis X. Weiser

LUCY, whose day is in our darkest season,
(Although your name is full of light,)
We walkers in the murk and rain of flesh and sense,
Lost in the midnight of our dead world's winter solstice
Look for the fogs to open on your friendly star.

We have long since cut down the summer of history;
Our cheerful towns have all gone out
     like fireflies in October.
The fields are flooded and the vine is bare:
How have our long days dwindled,
     now the world is frozen!

Locked in the cold jails of our stubborn will,
Oh hear the shovels growling in the gravel.
This is the way they'll make our beds for ever,
Ours, whose Decembers have put out the sun:
Doors of whose souls are shut against the summertime!

Martyr, whose short day sees our winter and our Calvary,
Show us some light, who seem forsaken by the sky:
We have so dwelt in darkness that our eyes are screened
     and dim,
And all but blinded by the weakest ray.

Hallow the vespers and December of our life,
     O martyred Lucy:
Console our solstice with your friendly day.   Thomas Merton

MY candle burns at both ends;
It will not last the night;
But ah, my foes, and oh, my friends—
It gives a lovely light!   Edna St. Vincent
                                           Millay

MASTER of the universe, know that the children of Israel are suffering too much; they deserve redemption, they need it. But if, for reasons unknown to me, you are not willing, not yet, then redeem all the other nations, but do it soon!

Hasidic tale told by Elie Wiesel

RORATE caeli desuper, et nubes pluant justum. Aperiatur terra, et germinet Salvatorem.

Rain down your dew, you heavens,
and you clouds, rain down the just one.
Earth, be opened,
and give birth to the Savior.

Monastic liturgy

NOW burn, new born to the world,
Double-natured name,
The heaven-flung, heart-fleshed, maiden-furled
Miracle-in-Mary-of-flame,
Mid-numbered He in three of the thunder-throne!
Not a dooms-day dazzle in his coming
nor dark as he came;
Kind, but royally reclaiming his own;
A released shower, let flash to the shire, not a lightning
of fire hard-hurled.

Gerard Manley Hopkins
Nineteenth century

B E kind to your land,
O Lord;
Bring to an end Jacob's exile.
Remove the guilt of your people;
Forgive them all their sins.
Stop being angry with us,
Turn away from your fiery wrath.
Restore us, our saving God,
And cease to rage against us.
Will you fume at us forever,
Staying angry, age after age?
If only you would restore us to life,
And let your people rejoice in you!
Show us your constant love, O Lord,
And offer us your salvation.

Let me hear what God declares,
For the Lord is declaring peace:
"I tell the people devoted to me,
Do not be complacent again!
For those who fear me, salvation is near;
My glory will dwell in your land."
Devotion and faith join together;
Peace and justice exchange a kiss.
Fidelity sprouts from the earth,
And justice looks down from the sky.
Surely the Lord will send rain,
And our land will produce the harvest.
Justice will come from God's presence,
And beauty will follow justice.   Psalm 85

THEN Judas Maccabeus and his brothers said, "Now that our enemies have been crushed, let us go up to purify the sanctuary and rededicate it." So the whole army assembled, and went up to Mount Zion. They found the sanctuary desolated, the altar desecrated, the gates burnt, weeds growing in the courts as in a forest or some mountain, and the priests' chambers demolished. Then they tore their clothes and made great lamentation; they sprinkled their heads with ashes and fell with their faces to the ground. And when the signal was given with trumpets, they cried out to Heaven.

Early in the morning on the twenty-fifth day of the ninth month, that is, the month of Chislev, in the year one hundred and forty-eight, they arose and offered sacrifice according to the law on the new altar of holocausts that they had made. On the anniversary of the day on which the Gentiles had defiled it, on that very day it was reconsecrated with songs, harps, flutes and cymbals. All the people prostrated themselves and adored and praised Heaven, who had given them success.

For eight days they celebrated the dedication of the altar and joyfully offered holocausts and sacrifices of deliverance and praise. They ornamented the facade of the temple with gold crowns and shields; they repaired the gates and the priests' chambers and furnished them with doors. There was great joy among the people now that the disgrace of the Gentiles was removed. Then Judas and his brothers and the entire congregation of Israel decreed that the days of the dedication of the altar should be observed with joy and gladness on the anniversary every year for eight days, from the twenty-fifth day of the month of Chislev.

1 Maccabees 4:36–40, 52–59

THE lights of Chanukah are a symbol of our joy. In time of darkness, our ancestors had the courage to struggle for freedom: freedom to be themselves, freedom to worship in their own way. Theirs was a victory of the weak over the strong, the few over the many, and the righteous over the arrogant. It was a victory for all ages and all peoples.

Blessed is the match consumed in kindling flame.
Blessed is the flame that burns in the heart's secret places.
Blessed is the heart with strength to stop its beating
    for honor's sake.
Blessed is the match consumed in kindling flame.

Within living memory, our people was plunged into deepest darkness. But we endured; the light of faith still burns brightly, and once again we see kindled the flame of freedom. Our people Israel has survived all who sought to destroy us. Now, through love and self-sacrifice, we labor to renew our life.

Let the lights we kindle shine forth for the world. May they illumine our lives even as they fill us with gratitude that our faith has been saved from extinction time and again.

We kindle these lights because of the wondrous deliverance you performed for our ancestors.

During these eight days of Chanukah these lights are sacred; we are not to use them but only to behold them, so that their glow may rouse us to give thanks for Your wondrous acts of deliverance.

Jewish prayerbook

B ARUCH atta, Adonai,
Elohenu melech ha-olam,
shehecheyanu v'kiyemanu
v'higianu laz'man hazeh.

Blessed is the Lord our God, ruler of the universe,
for you have kept us in life, sustained us,
and brought us to this holy season.

Jewish prayerbook

S UPER te Jerusalem orietur Dominus,
et gloria ejus in te videbitur.

Above you the Lord shall rise, Jerusalem,
and in you the glory of the Lord will shine.

Monastic liturgy

THE beginning of the gospel of Jesus Christ, the Son of God.

As it is written in Isaiah the prophet,
"Behold, I send my messenger before your face,
who shall prepare your way;
the voice of one crying in the wilderness:
Prepare the way of the Lord,
make straight the paths of the Lord—"

John the baptizer appeared in the wilderness, preaching a baptism of repentance for the forgiveness of sins. And there went out to him all the country of Judea, and all the people of Jerusalem; and they were baptized by him in the river Jordan, confessing their sins. Now John was clothed with camel's hair, and had a leather belt around his waist, and ate locusts and wild honey. And he preached, saying, "After me comes one who is mightier than I, the thong of whose sandals I am not worthy to stoop down and untie. I have baptized you with water; but the one who is coming will baptize you with the Holy Spirit."

Mark 1:1–8

REJOICE in the Lord always. I shall say it again: rejoice! Your kindness should be known to all. The Lord is near. Have no anxiety at all.

Philippians 4:4–5

ON Jordan's bank the Baptist's cry
Announces that the Lord is nigh;
Awake and hearken, for he brings
Glad tidings of the King of kings.

Then cleansed be ev'ry heart from sin;
Make straight the way for God within,
And let each heart prepare a home
Where such a mighty guest may come.

For you are our salvation, Lord,
Our refuge, and our great reward;
Without your grace we waste away
Like flow'rs that wither and decay.

To heal our sick stretch out your hand,
And bid the fallen sinner stand;
Shine forth, and let your light restore
Earth's own true loveliness once more.

All praise the Son eternally
Whose advent sets his people free;
Whom with the Father we adore
And Spirit blest for evermore.

Charles Coffin
Eighteenth century

THE Spirit of the Lord GOD is upon me,
    because the LORD has anointed me
to bring good tidings to the afflicted;
    the LORD has sent me to bind up the brokenhearted,
to proclaim liberty to the captives,
    and the opening of the prison to those who are bound;
to proclaim the year of the LORD's favor,
    and the day of vengeance of our God;
    to comfort all who mourn;
to grant to those who mourn in Zion—
    to give them a garland instead of ashes,
the oil of gladness instead of mourning,
    the mantle of praise instead of a faint spirit;
that they may be called oaks of righteousness,
    the planting of the LORD, that God may be glorified.

I will greatly rejoice in the LORD,
    my soul shall exult in my God;
for God has clothed me with the garments of salvation,
    and covered me with the robe of righteousness,

as a bridegroom decks himself with a garland,
    and as a bride adorns herself with her jewels.
For as the earth brings forth its shoots,
    and as a garden causes what is sown in it to spring up,
so the Lord GOD will cause righteousness and praise
    to spring forth before all the nations.

Isaiah 61:1–3, 10–11

Paul wrote: "Is it possible that I, an Israelite, descended from Abraham through the tribe of Benjamin, could agree that God had rejected this people?" He then likens the Gentile Christians (us) to a wild branch grafted to a tree that is Israel. "Remember," he says, "it is the root that supports *you.*"

Remember. But we forgot. We took a Jewish prophet like Isaiah and decided he could only be talking about Jesus. And with all those clear prophecies, how could the Jews have missed the Messiah? And Christians got into a habit of drawing old/new comparisons: the old way of the Jews being empty and sour, all in contrast to our shining selves.

Advent makes us face this. Our generation must do so with the Holocaust as witness. We can love Isaiah as a Jewish prophet talking to Jews, still. Vatican II taught that the writings of the prophets have their own value, entirely apart from the New Testament. And John Paul II has affirmed— along with the apostle Paul—that God's covenant with the Jews is a living reality.

What then of these Advent readings from Isaiah? Try reading Isaiah in light of what the Vatican Commission on Religious Relations with the Jews wrote: "Attentive to the same God who has spoken, hanging on the same word, we Jews and Christians have to witness to one same memory and one common hope to the one who is master of history. We must also accept our responsibility to prepare the world for the coming of the Messiah by working together for social justice."

Gabe Huck   To prepare the world for the coming of *whom*? And how?

E LEVARE, elevare, consurge Jerusalem:
solve vincula colli tui, captiva filia Sion.

Arise, Jerusalem, stand tall!
Daughter Sion, throw off the harness
  that keeps you prisoner.

Monastic liturgy

T HE end of all things is at hand. Therefore, be serious and
sober for prayers. Above all, let your love for one
another be intense, because love covers a multitude of sins.   1 Peter 4:7–8

W HEN first I heard his voice, I wakened
drowning in my mother.

She stooped and touched my eyes.
Womb, desert, dungeon, light and dark.

Then. A sword forbade me to grow old; it cut
time like a parasite from eternity.

Could death have eyed and pierced my body, could I
have stood upon the nails an hour,
would he take warning from his murdered shade
casting his fate in smoky runes
with points of light
like lips where death had fastened?

I follow from sad limbo
till death unfasten, till his rising
unwind and wear me
aureole   choir   crown.   Daniel Berrigan

L O, I am sending my messenger
to prepare the way before me;
And suddenly there will come to the temple
the LORD whom you seek,
And the messenger of the covenant whom you desire.

Malachi 3:1   Yes, he is coming, says the LORD of hosts.

A S they were coming down from the mountain, the disciples asked Jesus: "Why do the scribes say that Elijah must come first?" He said in reply: "Elijah will indeed come and restore all things; but I tell you that Elijah has already come." Then the disciples understood that he was
Matthew 17:10–12, 13   speaking to them of John the Baptist.

H AIR of the camel furnished a coarse raiment
To your blessed members; leather your girdle;
You drink the cold spring, food for you wild honey
Mingled with locusts.

All other prophets, in their hearts divining,
Sang of the light coming to the people;
Your finger touched the Lamb of God who takes
Sin from the world.

None has arisen in the mighty spaces
Of round earth's borders holier than John was:
Paul, deacon
of Apulia   Great was his grace who poured the mystic waters
Eighth century   O'er the Redeemer.

L IKE a fire there appeared the prophet Elijah
  whose words were as a flaming furnace.
Their staff of bread he shattered,
   in his zeal he reduced them to straits;
By God's word he shut up the heavens
   and three times brought down fire.
How awesome are you, Elijah!
   Whose glory is equal to yours?
You were taken aloft in a whirlwind,
   in a chariot with fiery horses.
You are destined, it is written, in time to come
   to put an end to wrath before the day of the LORD,
To turn back the hearts of parents toward their children,
   and to reestablish the tribes of Jacob.
Blessed [are those who shall see you before they die],
   O Elijah, enveloped in the whirlwind.   Sirach 48:1–4, 9–12

L O, I will send you
  Elijah, the prophet,
Before the day of the LORD comes,
   the great and terrible day.   Malachi 3:23

O God, whose will is justice for the poor
   and peace for the afflicted,
let your herald's urgent voice
pierce our hardened hearts
and announce the dawn of your kingdom.
Before the advent of the one who baptizes
with the fire of the Holy Spirit,
let our complacency give way to conversion,
oppression to justice,

and conflict to acceptance of one another in Christ.
We ask this through him whose coming is certain,
whose day draws near:
your Son, our Lord Jesus Christ,
who lives and reigns with you and the Holy Spirit,
one God, for ever and ever.

Prayer,
Second Sunday
of Advent

THIS is the dead land
This is the cactus land
Here the stone images
Are raised, here they receive
The supplication of a dead man's hand
Under the twinkle of a fading star.

Is it like this
In death's other kingdom
Walking alone
At the hour when we are
Trembling with tenderness
Lips that would kiss
Form prayers to broken stone.

T. S. Eliot

COMFORT, give comfort to my people,
says your God.
Speak tenderly to Jerusalem, and proclaim to her
that her service is at an end,
her guilt is expiated;
Indeed, she has received from the hand of the Lord
double for all her sins.

Isaiah 40:1–2

Y OU must be men and women of ceaseless hope, because only tomorrow can today's human and Christian promise be realized; and every tomorrow will have its own tomorrow, world without end. Every human act, every Christian act, is an act of hope. But that means you must be men and women of the present, you must live this moment—really live it, not just endure it—because this very moment, for all its imperfection and frustration, *because* of its imperfection and frustration, is pregnant with all sorts of possibilities, is pregnant with the future, is pregnant with love, is pregnant with Christ.

Walter J. Burghardt

N OTHING that is worth doing can be achieved in our lifetime; therefore we must be saved by hope. Nothing which is true or beautiful or good makes complete sense in any immediate context of history; therefore we must be saved by faith. Nothing we do, however virtuous, can be accomplished alone; therefore we must be saved by love. No virtuous act is quite as virtuous from the standpoint of our friend or foe as it is from our standpoint. Therefore we must be saved by the final form of love which is forgiveness.

Reinhold Niebuhr

G ET you up to a high mountain,
O Zion, herald of glad tidings;
lift up your voice with strength,
    O Jerusalem, herald of good tidings,
    lift it up, fear not;
say to the cities of Judah:
    "Behold your God!"
Behold, the Lord GOD comes with might,
    with an arm to rule;
behold, God comes bearing the reward,
    preceded by the recompense.

The LORD will feed the chosen flock like a shepherd;
God's arms will gather the lambs.
God's bosom will bear them up;

Isaiah 40:9–11   the LORD will gently lead those that are with young.

L AETAMINI cum Jerusalem,
et exsultate in ea omnes qui diligitis eam in aeternum.

Share the mirth of Jerusalem and dance in her streets,

Monastic liturgy   all of you whose love for her lasts forever.

W HEN the great Rabbi Israel Baal Shem-Tov saw misfortune threatening the Jews it was his custom to go into a certain part of the forest to meditate. There he would light a fire, say a special prayer, and the miracle would be accomplished and misfortune averted.

Later, when his disciple, the celebrated Magid of Mezritch, had occasion, for the same reason, to intercede with heaven, he would go to the same place in the forest and say: "Master of the Universe, listen! I do not know how to light the fire, but I am still able to say the prayers." And again the miracle would be accomplished.

Still later, Rabbi Moshe-Leib of Sasov, in order to save his people once more, would go into the forest and say: "I do not know how to light the fire, I do not know the prayer, but I know the place and this must be sufficient." It was sufficient and the miracle was accomplished.

Then it fell to Rabbi Israel of Rizhyn to overcome misfortune. Sitting in his armchair, his head in his hands, he spoke to

God: "I am unable to light the fire and I do not know the prayer; I cannot even find the place in the forest. All I can do is to tell the story, and that must be sufficient." And it was sufficient. God made humankind because God loves stories.

Hasidic tale told by
Elie Wiesel

I fled Him, down the nights and down the days;
I fled Him, down the arches of the years;
I fled Him, down the labyrinthine ways
  Of my own mind; and in the mist of tears
I hid from Him, and under running laughter.

Francis Thompson
Nineteenth century

LATE have I loved you, O Beauty so ancient and so new; late have I loved you. For behold you were within me, and I outside; and I sought you outside and in my unloveliness fell upon those lovely things that you have made. You were with me, and I was not with you. I was kept from you by those things, yet had they not been in you, they would not have been at all. You called and cried to me to break open my deafness and you sent forth your beams and you shone upon me and chased away my blindness. You breathed fragrance upon me, and I drew in my breath and do now pant for you. I tasted you, and now hunger and thirst for you. You touched me, and I have burned for your peace.

Augustine
Fifth century

BUT you have seen the trouble and sorrow,
you note it, you take it in hand.
The helpless entrust themselves to you,
for you are the helper of the orphan.

Psalm 10:14

EXSPECTETUR sicut pluvia eloquium Domini:
et descendet super nos sicut ros Deus noster.

We wait for the word of the Lord as we wait for the rains
and our God shall come down upon us like gentle dew.

Monastic liturgy

A voice cries out:
In the desert prepare the way of the LORD!
Make straight in the wasteland a highway for our God!
Every valley shall be filled in,
    every mountain and hill shall be made low;
The rugged land shall be made a plain,
    the rough country, a broad valley.
Then the glory of the LORD shall be revealed,
    and all humankind shall see it together;
Isaiah 40:3–5   for the mouth of the LORD has spoken.

HOPE is the presentiment that the imagination is more
real, and reality less real, than we had thought. It is the
sensation that the last word does not belong to the brutality
of facts with their oppression and repression. It is the suspi-
cion that reality is far more complex than realism would
have us believe, that the frontiers of the possible are not
determined by the limits of the present, and that miracu-
lously and surprisingly, life is readying the creative event that
Rubem Alves   will open the way to freedom and resurrection.

I have a dream today. I have a dream that one day "every valley shall be exalted, every hill and mountain shall be made low, and the rough places will be made plains, and the crooked places will be made straight, and the glory of the Lord shall be revealed, and all flesh shall see it together."

This is our hope. This is the faith that I go back to the South with. With this faith we will be able to hew out of the mountain of despair a stone of hope. With this faith we will be able to transform the jangling discords of our nation into a beautiful symphony of brotherhood. With this faith we will be able to work together, to pray together, to struggle together, to stand up for freedom together, knowing that we will be free one day.

And when this happens, and when we allow freedom to ring, when we let it ring from every village and every hamlet, from every state and every city, we will be able to speed up that day when all God's children, black and white, Jews and Gentiles, Protestants and Catholics, will be able to join hands and sing the words of that old Negro spiritual, "Free at last! Free at last! Thank God almighty, we are free at last!"   Martin Luther King, Jr.

O DAY of peace that dimly shines
Through all our hopes and prayers and dreams,
Guide us to justice, truth and love;
Delivered from our selfish schemes.
May swords of hate fall from our hands,
Our hearts from envy find release,
Till by God's grace our warring world
Shall see Christ's promised reign of peace.

Then shall the wolf dwell with the lamb
Nor shall the fierce devour the small;
As beasts and cattle calmly graze,
A little child shall lead them all.
Then enemies shall learn to love,

All creatures find their true accord;
The hope of peace shall be fulfilled,
For all the earth shall know the Lord.

Carl P. Daw, Jr.

F ATHER of our Lord Jesus Christ,
ever faithful to your promises
and ever close to your church:
the earth rejoices in hope of the Savior's coming
and looks forward with longing
to his return at the end of time.
Prepare our hearts and remove the sadness
that hinders us from feeling the joy and hope
which his presence will bestow,
for he is Lord for ever and ever.

Roman rite

I believe with all my belief
in the coming of the messiah.
And even if there is a delay,
I believe.

Hebrew song

T HERE is a divine dream which the prophets and rabbis
have cherished and which fills our prayers, and permeates the acts of true piety. It is the dream of a world, rid of evil by the grace of God as well as by [our] efforts . . . to the task of establishing the kingship of God in the world. God is waiting for us to redeem the world. We should not spend our life hunting for trivial satisfactions while God is waiting constantly and keenly for our effort and devotion.

The Almighty has not created the universe that we may have opportunities to satisfy our greed, envy and ambition. We have not survived that we may waste our years in vulgar vanities. The martyrdom of millions demands that we consecrate ourselves to the fulfillment of God's dream of salvation. Israel did not accept the Torah of their own free will. When Israel approached Sinai, God lifted up the mountain and

held it over their heads, saying: "Either you accept the Torah
or be crushed beneath the mountain."

The mountain of history is over our heads again. Shall we
renew the covenant with God?   Abraham Heschel

M ONTES et colles cantabunt coram Deo laudem,
   et omnia ligna silvarum plaudent manibus:
quoniam veniet Dominus Dominator
et regnum aeternum, alleluia.

The hills and the mountains will be singing praise to God.
Every tree in the forest will be clapping its hands.
The Lord will come and rule forever. Alleluia.   Monastic liturgy

F ATHER, all-powerful and ever-living God,
   we do well always and everywhere to give you thanks
through Jesus Christ our Lord.
His future coming was proclaimed by all the prophets.
The virgin mother bore him in her womb
with love beyond all telling.
John the Baptist was his herald
and made him known when at last he came.
In his love Christ has filled us with joy
as we prepare to celebrate his birth,
so that when he comes he may find us watching in prayer,
our hearts filled with wonder and praise.   Roman rite

W E live always during Advent. We are always waiting
   for the messiah to come. The messiah has come, but
is not yet fully manifest. The messiah is not fully manifest in
each of our souls, not fully manifest in humankind as a
whole: that is to say, that just as Christ was born according to
the flesh in Bethlehem of Judah, so must he be born according to the spirit in each of our souls.   Jean Danielou

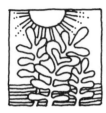

THE wilderness and the dry land shall be glad,
    the desert shall rejoice and blossom;
like the crocus it shall blossom abundantly,
    and rejoice with joy and singing.
The glory of Lebanon shall be given to it,
    the majesty of Carmel and Sharon.
They shall see the glory of the LORD,
    the majesty of our God.
Strengthen the weak hands,
    and make firm the feeble knees.
Say to those who are of a fearful heart,
    "Be strong, fear not!
Behold, your God
    will come with vengeance,
with the recompense of God.
    God will come and save you."
Then the eyes of the blind shall be opened,
    and the ears of the deaf unstopped;
then shall the lame leap like a hart,
    and the tongue of the dumb sing for joy.
For the waters shall break forth in the wilderness,
    and streams in the desert;
the burning sand shall become a pool,
    and the thirsty ground springs of water;
the haunt of jackals shall become a swamp,
    the grass shall become reeds and rushes.
And a highway shall be there,
    and it shall be called the Holy Way;
the unclean shall not pass over it,
    and fools shall not err therein.
No lion shall be there,
    nor shall any ravenous beast come upon it;
they shall not be found there,

but the redeemed shall walk there.
And the ransomed of the LORD shall return,
   and come to Zion with singing;
   everlasting joy shall be upon their heads;
   they shall obtain joy and gladness,
   and sorrow and sighing shall flee away.   Isaiah 35:1–10

JUSTE et pie vivamus, exspectantes beatam spem,
   et adventum Domini.

Let us live by justice and by mercy
and wait with bright hope for the Lord to come.   Monastic liturgy

WHY, O Jacob, do you say,
      and declare, O Israel,
"My way is hidden from the LORD,
   and my right is disregarded by my God"?
Do you not know
   or have you not heard?
The LORD is the eternal God,
   creator of the ends of the earth.
They that hope in the LORD will renew their strength,
   they will soar as with eagles' wings;
They will run and not grow weary,
   walk and not grow faint.   Isaiah 40:27–28, 31

IF you think you can bring your people back into the fold
   by making them suffer, then I, Leib, son of Rachel, swear
to you that you will not succeed. So why try? Save your chil-
dren by giving them joy, by delivering them. By doing it that   Hasidic tale told by
way, you have nothing to lose and everything to gain.   Elie Wiesel

CONSOLAMINI, consolamini, populé meus,
dicit Deus vester.

Your God speaks:

Monastic liturgy   Comfort, take comfort, my people.

Irenaeus of Lyons   THE glory of God is a living person and the life of each
Second century   living person is the vision of God.

THUS says the Lord GOD,
the Holy One of Israel:
O people of Zion, who dwell in Jerusalem,
   no more will you weep.
The Lord will give you the bread you need
   and the water for which you thirst.
No longer will your Teacher hide,
   but with your own eyes you shall see your Teacher,
While from behind, a voice shall sound in your ears:
   "This is the way; walk in it,"
   when you would turn to the right or to the left.
[The LORD] will give rain for the seed
   that you sow in the ground,
And the wheat that the soil produces
   will be rich and abundant.
On that day your cattle will graze
   in spacious meadows;
The oxen and the asses that till the ground
   will eat silage tossed to them
   with shovel and pitchfork.
Upon every high mountain and lofty hill

there will be streams of running water.
On the day of the great slaughter,
    when the towers fall,
The light of the moon will be like that of the sun
    and the light of the sun will be seven times greater
    like the light of seven days.

Isaiah 30:19–21,
23–26

OIL, passing along the banks of Lake Maracaibo, has taken away the colors. In this Venezuelan garbage dump of sordid streets, dirty air and oily waters, Rafael Vargas lives and paints.

Grass does not grow in Cabimas, dead city, emptied land, nor do fish remain in its waters, nor birds in its air, nor roosters in its dawns; but in Vargas's paintings the world is in fiesta, the earth breathes at the top of its lungs, the greenest of trees burst with fruit and flowers, and prodigious fish, birds, and roosters jostle one another like people.

Vargas hardly knows how to read or write. He does know how to earn a living as a carpenter, and how as a painter to earn the clean light of his days: His is the revenge, the prophecy of one who paints not the reality he knows but the reality he needs.

Eduardo Galeano

OUR brokenness is the wound through which the full power of God
can penetrate our being
and transfigure us in God.

Loneliness is not something from which we must flee
but the place from where we can cry out to God,
where God will find us and we can find God.

Yes, through our wounds
the power of God can penetrate us
and become like rivers of living water
to irrigate the arid earth within us.
Thus we may irrigate the arid earth of others,
Jean Vanier   so that hope and love are reborn.

S EE how the farmer waits for the precious fruit of the earth,
being patient with it until it receives the early and the late
rains. You too must be patient. Make your hearts firm,
James 5:7–8   because the coming of the Lord is at hand.

R ISE up, Lord, with mercy for Sion,
for the time of mercy has come,
Cistercian liturgy   the time has come at last.

A legend tells that when the almighty Lord
Proclaimed to Moses his eternal word,
He in a vision showed to him likewise
The treasures that lie stored in Paradise.
And at each one in turn the heavenly voice
Spake: "This the treasure is, that shall rejoice
His soul who freely giveth alms, and here
His portion is who dries the orphan's tear."
Thus one by one were all to him made known,
Until unnamed remained but one alone.
Then Moses said: "I pray thee, what is this?"
And answer made the Lord most High: "It is
The treasure of my mercy, freely given
Talmudic legend   To those who else were treasureless in heaven."

BEHOLD, I am coming soon, bringing my recompense, to repay all for what they have done. I am the Alpha and the Omega, the first and the last, the beginning and the end."

Blessed are those who wash their robes, that they may have the right to the tree of life and that they may enter the city by the gates.

"I, Jesus, have sent my angel to you with this testimony for the churches. I am the root and the offspring of David, the bright morning star."

The Spirit and the Bride say, "Come." And let the hearer say, "Come." And let the thirsty come, let the one who desires take the water of life without price.

The one who testifies to these things says, "Surely I am coming soon." Amen. Come, Lord Jesus!

Revelation 22:12–14, 16–17, 20

YOU believe that the Son of God once came to us;
you look for him to come again.
May his coming bring you the light of his holiness
and free you with his blessing.

May God make you steadfast in faith,
joyful in hope, and untiring in love
all the days of your life.

You rejoice that our Redeemer came to live with us
as one of us.
When he comes again in glory,
may he reward you with endless life.

Roman rite

F OR it is truly meet and right, proper and healthful, that we should always give thanks to you, here and everywhere, O holy Lord, Father almighty, everlasting God, through Christ our Lord, by whose incarnation the world's salvation was accomplished, by whose passion the redemption of the children of humankind was procured. May he himself, we beseech you, conduct us to the eternal reward, who redeemed us from the darkness of hell: and may he justify us at his second coming, who redeemed us in his first: that his exaltation may defend us from all evil, whose humiliation has raised us to life: through whom the angels
Ambrosian rite   praise your majesty.

B ECAUSE the beginning shall remind us of the end
T. S. Eliot   And the first coming of the second coming.

T O listen—in faith—to find one's way and have the feeling that, under God, one is really finding it again.

This is like playing blindman's buff:
deprived of sight, I have, in compensation, to
sharpen all my other senses, to grope my way and
recognize myself as I pass my fingers over the
faces of my friends, and thus find what was
mine already and had been there all the time. What
I would have known all the time was there, had I
Dag Hammarskjöld   not blindfolded myself.

R EBBE Barukh's grandson, Yehiel, came running into his study in tears. "Yehiel, Yehiel, why are you crying?"

"My friend cheats! It's unfair; he left me all by myself, that's why I am crying."

"Would you like to tell me about it?"

"Certainly, Grandfather. We played hide-and-seek, and it was my turn to hide and his turn to look for me. So he gave up; he stopped looking. And that's unfair."

Rebbe Barukh began to caress Yehiel's face, and tears welled up in his eyes. "God too, Yehiel," he whispered softly. "God too is unhappy; he is hiding and man is not looking for him. Do you understand, Yehiel? God is hiding and man is not even searching for him."

Hasidic tale told by Elie Wiesel

O N that day
    You need not be ashamed
  of all your deeds,
    your rebellious actions against me;
For then will I remove from your midst
    the proud braggarts,
And you shall no longer exalt yourself
    on my holy mountain.
But I will leave as a remnant in your midst
    a people humble and lowly,
Who shall take refuge in the name of the LORD:
    the remnant of Israel.
They shall do no wrong
    and speak no lies;
Nor shall there be found in their mouths
    a deceitful tongue;
They shall pasture and couch their flocks
    with none to disturb them.

Zephaniah 3:11–13

THAT of which the season of the year and our customary devotion reminds us, we, Dearly Beloved, in our paternal duty, now preach to you. You must observe the fast of the tenth month [December], whereby, for the complete harvest of all fruits, there is most fittingly offered to God, the giver of them, an offering of self mortification. For what can be more salutary for us than fasting, by the practice of which we draw nigh to God, and, standing fast against the devil, defeat the vices that lead us astray.

For fasting was ever the food of virtue. From abstinence there arise chaste thoughts, just decisions, salutary counsels. And through voluntary suffering the flesh dies to the concupiscences, and the spirit waxes strong in virtue. But as the salvation of our souls is not gained solely by fasting, let us fill up what is wanting in our fasting with almsgiving to the poor. Let us give to virtue what we take from pleasure. Let the abstinence of those who fast be the dinner of the poor.

Let us have thought for the protection of the widow, for the welfare of the orphan, for the comforting of those who mourn, for the peace of those who live in discord. Let the stranger be given shelter. Let the oppressed be aided, the naked be clothed, the sick cherished.

Leo
Fifth century

THUS says the LORD of hosts: Old men and old women, each with staff in hand because of old age, shall again sit in the streets of Jerusalem. The city shall be filled with boys and girls playing in the streets. Thus says the LORD of hosts: Even if this should seem impossible in the eyes of the remnant of this people, shall it in those days be impossible in my eyes also, says the LORD of hosts? Thus says the LORD of hosts: Lo, I will rescue my people from the land of the rising sun, and from the land of the setting sun. I will bring them back to dwell within Jerusalem. They shall be my people, and I will be their God, with faithfulness and justice.

This word of the LORD of hosts came to me: Thus says the LORD of hosts: The fast days of the fourth, the fifth, the seventh, and the tenth months shall become occasions of joy and gladness, cheerful festivals for the house of Judah; only love faithfulness and peace. Thus says the LORD of hosts: There shall yet come peoples, the inhabitants of many cities; and the inhabitants of one city shall approach those of another, and say, "Come! Let us go to implore the favor of the LORD"; and, "I too will go to seek the LORD." Many people and strong nations shall come to seek the LORD of hosts in Jerusalem and to implore the favor of the LORD. Thus says the LORD of hosts: In those days ten people of every nationality, speaking different tongues, shall take hold of, yes, take hold of every Jew by the edge of the garment and say, "Let us go with you, for we have heard that God is with you."

Zechariah 8:4–8, 18–23

B UT what would our spirits be, O God, if they did not have the bread of earthly things to nourish them, the wine of created beauties to intoxicate them, and the conflicts of human life to fortify them?

Pierre Teilhard de Chardin

O NCE two brothers went to visit an old man. It was not the old man's habit, however, to eat every day. When he saw the brothers, he welcomed them with joy, and said: "Fasting has its own reward, but if you eat for the sake of love you satisfy two commandments, for you give up your own will and also fulfill the commandment to refresh others."

Desert Wisdom

L AS Posadas, literally, "the shelters," which begins on the 16th of December, is celebrated with great joy as the "holy pilgrims" (Mary and Joseph) move each night from house to house, one after another. It is always celebrated with song, prayers and special food, some of which are: tamales, donuts, champurrado and buffets.

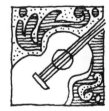

Why? Because it is the time of Advent, the time of expectation, the jubilant wait, the time when all await the birth of the son, awaiting the celebration of his birthday. This is the time of Las Posadas, the time of joy, preparation and waiting.

Why do people carry lanterns in the procession of Las Posadas? Because all those carrying the lanterns represent the stars which illuminate the way for the shepherds who make their way to the house of the birth.

Celestina Castro

F OR the LORD, your God, befriends the alien, feeding and clothing them. So you too must befriend the alien, for you were once aliens yourselves.

Deuteronomy
10:17–19

D IVINO y eterno Verbo, que desde el Padre descendiste al corazón de siempre Virgen María; el amor que tienes a los hombres te conduce a la ciudad de Belén para nacer a media noche en un pobre y humilde establo.

Es verdad que millares de ángeles te acompañan en este viaje; pero también es cierto que te dejamos, nosotros a quienes viniste a salvar y a conducir al Belén de la eterna felicidad.

Perdónanos, Dios y Señor del Universo, y ayúdanos a caminar con María y San José para luchar y poder triunfar sobre toda adversidad. Amén.

Divine and eternal Word, who descended from the Father into the heart of the ever Virgin Mary, your love for humankind leads you to Bethlehem where you are born at midnight in a poor and humble stable.

In truth, thousands of angels accompany you on this journey, and yet we, whom you came to save and lead to that Bethlehem of eternal joy, stubbornly turn away from you.

Forgive us, God and Lord of the universe, and help us to walk alongside Mary and Joseph, thus giving us the courage to fight against and triumph over every adversity. Amen.

Posadas prayer

L AS Posadas is a time of celebration in Mexico and the Southwest United States. It is an event of much significance with joy, protection and festivity. Las Posadas is always observed with much song and celebration. It is a novena of preparation for the feast of the Nativity. It begins on the 16th of December and ends on the 24th of December with the "Mass of the Rooster," the celebration of the Mass at Midnight.

Las Posadas has its origins, possibly, from Father Diego de Soria, a religious of the order of St. Augustine. He was an enthusiastic priest, introducing the devotion in Mexico, in the church of Alcoman, in 1587. It was the intention of this celebrated religious to contrast the celebration of the Aztecs in honor of their god of war, Huitzilopochtli. It was celebrated at the same time as the time of the Nativity, and was presenting many problems of attraction for the neophyte Christians.

Las Posadas of Father Diego became popular very quickly and extended to other churches in Mexico and the surrounding countryside. It then began to be celebrated in the homes of individuals.

It is the celebration of the "pilgrims" who go from house to house led by an angel who conducts the little donkey with the seated Virgin. She is accompanied by St. Joseph. They sing songs as they look for shelter, the masters of the houses open their doors and all who participate share in the buffet which the owners (innkeepers) of the house offer.

The people celebrate that the messiah will come again. It is the celebration of preparation for this coming. It is time to open the doors of our hearts to give shelter. How do we give shelter to Jesus? By the doing of good works. It is the preparation time for the doing and practicing of the virtues. It is a time for coming together with our neighbors. It is the occasion for gathering with our families and with those who live near us.

Fiestas Navideñas

WHILE we may be sure that the Advent season developed first outside of Rome, to say more than that is not as easy as one might wish. Usener suggested, as have many others, that we see the beginnings of Advent in the fourth canon of a Council of Saragossa in 380. That canon urges the constant presence of the faithful in the church, calling on them not to stay at home or run off to the country or the mountains during a period of twenty-one continuous days, beginning from December 17 and reaching to the Epiphany.

In spite of many shifts and changes, that date is still the most common for the beginning of the "Great O" antiphons that have characterized vespers (and perhaps lauds originally) during the latter days of Advent from perhaps as early as the seventh century.

Thomas Talley

Irenaeus of Lyons
Second century

LUKE shows that the genealogy which traces lineage from our Lord back to Adam comprises seventy-two generations. Thus the end is joined with the beginning and we are shown that it is he who has summed up in himself all the nations descended from Adam who are dispersed throughout the world, and all people of different languages. Together with Adam he has summed up all generations.

WHEN Jesus began his work he was about thirty years old. He was the son, so people thought, of Joseph, who was the son of Heli, the son of Matthat, the son of Levi, the son of Melchi, the son of Jannai, the son of Joseph, the son of Mattathias, the son of Amos, the son of Nahum, the

son of Esli, the son of Naggai, the son of Maath, the son of Mattathias, the son of Semein, the son of Josech, the son of Joda,
the son of Joanan, the son of Rhesa, the son of Zerubbabel,
the son of Shealtiel, the son of Neri, the son of Melchi, the
son of Addi, the son of Cosam, the son of Elmadam, the son
of Er, the son of Joshua, the son of Eliezer, the son of Jorim,
the son of Matthat, the son of Levi, the son of Simeon, the
son of Judah, the son of Joseph, the son of Jonam, the son of
Eliakim, the son of Melea, the son of Menna, the son of Mat-
tatha, the son of Nathan, the son of David, the son of Jesse,
the son of Obed, the son of Boaz, the son of Salmon, the son
of Nahshon, the son of Amminadab, the son of Admin, the
son of Arni, the son of Hezron, the son of Perez, the son of
Judah, the son of Jacob, the son of Isaac, the son of Abraham,
the son of Terah, the son of Nahor, the son of Serug, the son
of Reu, the son of Peleg, the son of Eber, the son of Shelah,
the son of Cainan, the son of Arphaxad, the son of Shem, the
son of Noah, the son of Lamech, the son of Methuselah, the
son of Enoch, the son of Jared, the son of Mahalaleel, the son
of Kenan, the son of Enosh, the son of Seth, the son of Adam,
the son of God.   Luke 3:23–38

C OME, O Feast-lovers, let us sing a hymn of praise to all
    the assembly of the ancestors: Adam, Enoch, Noah,
Melchisedech, Abraham, Isaac and Jacob, Moses, Aaron,
Josue and Samuel, Isaiah, Jeremiah, Ezekiel and Daniel,
Elijah and Elisha and all the other fathers; the holy women
made strong in the days of old by the might of your strength,
O Lord: Hannah, Judith, Deborah, Hulda, Jael, Esther,
Sarah, Miriam, Rachel, Rebecca, Ruth. You shone as
heaven's lights upon the earth, enkindling the light of piety.
You called forth the choir of all creation as you sang to the
one who saves all from temptation.   Orthodox liturgy

O Wisdom, O holy word of God,
  you govern all creation
with your strong yet tender care:
Vespers antiphon   Come and show your people the way to salvation.

O come, O Wisdom from on high,
  Who orders all things mightily;
Latin hymn   To us the path of knowledge show,
Ninth century   And teach us in her ways to go.

F ROM the mouth of the Most High I came forth,
  and mistlike covered the earth.
Before all ages, in the beginning, God created me,
  and through all ages I shall not cease to be.
Come to me, all you that yearn for me,
Sirach 24:3, 9, 18   and be filled with my fruits.

Y OU are the brightness of the Father's glory, the image of
  the one that begot you; you appeared in our human
flesh and enlightened our soul by the light of your life-giving
gospel. We praise and worship and glorify you at all times.
With your sacred wisdom make me wise, O Lord, and grant
that I may serve you by keeping your vivifying and divine
Malabarese rite   commandments, entirely and always. Amen.

THERE is one God, whose word and wisdom made and ordered all things. God's word is our Lord Jesus Christ who in these last times became human among humankind, that Christ might unite the end with the beginning, that is, humankind with God.

Irenaeus of Lyons
Second century

THE scribes wrote, "In the beginning God created. . . ." At first it was enough to give God's title, just "God," the God who is God, and to declare that God created the world. But language moves toward specificity: What we believe to be significant we distinguish linguistically from neighbors near and far. So the simple noun God was soon found to be meager, insufficient.

So to the question seeking discrimination, "But how did God create the world?" the ancient Hebrews sang a clarification: "God who by wisdom made the heavens, whose mercy endures for ever." (Psalm 136)

What is it about God that created the world? Wisdom. What did God use to create the world? Divine wisdom alone. Now we have a handle on this untouchable God: Wisdom. Why, we know about wisdom!—the workings of mind meshed with compassion. We can understand a little bit, at least, of God: Wisdom.

So much did divine wisdom occupy Hebrew imaginations that a figure is born, a mighty woman springing fully armed from the Hebrew poet's head: Lady Wisdom herself, whom God created first in the primeval time of creating. Lady Wisdom was God's companion, God's help, meet for creating the universe. The Hebrew writers prize her judgment, her stature, her beauty. This first-begotten of God stands by life's pathways and points us the way to her home in God. Later, Jews speaking Greek called her Sophia, the Wise Woman, a feminine personification of that essential attribute of omniscient God.

Gail Ramshaw

YOUR voice speaks:
In my arms I still carry flowers from the wilderness,
the dew on my hair is from the valleys of the dawn
of humankind.
I have prayers that the meadows lend an ear to, I know
how storms are tempered, how water is blest.
I carry in my womb the secrets of the desert, on my head
the noble web of ancient thought.
For I am mother to all Earth's children: why do you scorn
me, world, when my Heavenly Father makes me
so great?
Behold, in me long-vanished generations still kneel, and
out of my soul many pagans shine toward the infinite.
I lay hidden in the temples of their Gods, I was darkly
present in the sayings of their wise men.
I was on the towers with their star-gazers, I was with the
solitary women on whom the spirit descended.
I was the desire of all times, I was the light of all times,
I am the fullness of all times.
I am their great union, I am their eternal oneness.
I am the way of all their ways, on me the millennia are

Gertrude von le Fort   drawn to God.

THE Creator, the Wisdom of God, draws near,
The mist of the prophets' promise is dispersed.
Joy clears the skies,
Truth is resplendent,
The dark shadows are dispelled,
The gates of Eden are opened,
Adam dances in exultation:

Orthodox liturgy   Our Creator and God wills to fashion us anew.

O mother maiden! O gracious maiden mother!
O bush unburnt, burning in Moses' sight,
that ravished down from the diety
by your humility the spirit that alighted in you;
of whose virtue, when it lightened your heart,
the Father's wisdom was conceived.
Help me to tell it in reverence of you.

Lady, your bounty, your magnificence,
your virtue, and your great humility,
no tongue can express in any learned way;
for sometimes, Lady, before we pray to you,
you, in your benignity, anticipate them
and attain for us the light of your prayer
to guide us to your beloved Son.

So weak is my ability, O Blessed Queen,
to declare your great worthiness
that I cannot bear the weight,
but like a child of twelve months old or less,
who can hardly speak a word,
just so am I, and therefore I pray you: Geoffrey Chaucer
Guide the song which I shall speak of you.   Fourteenth century

O Lord, through your Son you command us, no, you
counsel us to ask, and you promise that you will hear
us so that our joy may be complete. Lord, I am making the
request that you urge us to make through your Wonder-
Counselor. Give me then what you promise to give through
your truth. You, O God, are faithful; grant that I may receive
my request, so that my joy may be complete.

Meanwhile, let this hope of mine be in my thoughts and on
my tongue; let my heart be filled with it, my voice speak of it;

Anselm
Eleventh century

let my soul hunger for it, my body thirst for it, my whole being yearn for it, until I enter into the joy of the Lord, who is Three in One, blessed for ever. Amen.

N OW the birth of Jesus Christ took place in this way. When his mother Mary had been betrothed to Joseph, before they came together she was found to be with child of the Holy Spirit; and her husband Joseph, being just, and unwilling to put her to shame, resolved to divorce her quietly. But as he considered this, behold, an angel of the Lord appeared to him in a dream, saying, "Joseph, son of David, do not fear to take Mary your wife, for that which is conceived in her is of the Holy Spirit; she will bear a son, and you shall call his name Jesus, for he will save his people from their sins." All this took place to fulfill what the Lord had spoken by the prophet:

"Behold, a virgin shall conceive and bear a son,
and his name shall be called Emmanuel"

(which means, God with us). When Joseph woke from sleep, he did as the angel of the Lord commanded him; he took Mary as his wife, but knew her not until she had borne a son; and he called his name Jesus.

Matthew 1:18–25

N OW the birth of Jesus Christ was on this wise: When as his mother Mary was espoused to Joseph, before they came together, she was found to be with child of the Holy Ghost. Then Joseph her husband, being a just man, and not willing to make her public example, was minded to put her away privily. But while he thought on these things, behold, the angel of the Lord appeared in a dream, saying, Joseph, thou son of David, fear not to take unto thee Mary thy wife: for that which is conceived in her is of the Holy Ghost. And she shall bring forth a son, and thou shalt call his name JESUS: for he shall save his people from their sins. Now all this was done, that it might be fulfilled which was spoken of the Lord by the prophet, saying, Behold, a virgin shall be with child, and shall bring forth a son, and they shall call his name Emmanuel, which being interpreted is, God with us.

Matthew 1:18–24
King James Version

M ERVELL nought, Josep, on Mary mylde;
Forsake hyr not tho she be with childe.

I, Josep, wonder how this may be,
That Mary wex gret when Y and she
Ever have levyd in chastite;
Iff she be with chylde, hit ys not by me.
   Mervell nought, Josep.
   Mervell nought, Josep.
The Holy Gost with mercifull disstens
In here hathe entryd withowte offens,
God and man conceyved by hys presens,
And she virgyn pure withowte violens.
   Mervell nought, Josep.
   Mervell nought, Josep.
What the angell of God to me dothe say
I, Josep, muste and will umble obay,
Ellys prively Y wolde have stole away,
But now will Y serve here tille that day.
   Mervell nought, Josep.
   Mervell nought, Josep.
Josep, thow shalt here mayde and moder fynde,
Here Sone redemptor of all mankynde
Thy forefaderes of paynes to unbynde;
Therefor muse not this matter in thy mynde.
   Mervell nought, Josep.
   Mervell nought, Josep.

English carol
Sixteenth century

IN the psalms of David,
in the words of the prophets,
in the dream of Joseph,
your promise is spoken, eternal God,
and takes flesh at last
in the womb of the Virgin.
May Emmanuel find welcome in our hearts,
take flesh in our lives, and be for all peoples
the welcome advent of redemption and grace.
We ask this through him whose coming is certain,
whose Day draws near:
your Son, our Lord Jesus Christ,
who lives and reigns with you and the Holy Spirit,
one God, for ever and ever.

Prayer,
Fourth Sunday
of Advent

JOSEPH: Now to Bedlam have we leagues three;
The day is nigh spent, it draweth toward night;
Fain at your ease, dame, I would that ye should be,
For you grow all weary, it seemeth in my sight.

Mary: God have mercy, Joseph, my spouse so dear;
All prophets hereto do bear witness,
The very time now draweth near
That my child will be born, which is King of bliss.

Unto some place, Joseph, hendly me lead,
That I might rest with grace in this tide.
The light of the Father over us both spread,
And the grace of my son with us here abide.

Joseph: Lo, blessed Mary, here shall ye lend
Chief chosen of our Lord and cleanest in degree;
And I for help to town will I wend.
Is not this the best, dame? What say ye?

Mary: God have mercy, Joseph, my husband so meek;
And heartily I pray you, go now from me.
Joseph: That shall be done in haste, Marý so sweet;
The comfort of the Holy Ghost leave I with thee.

Now to Bedlam straight will I wend
To get some help for Mary so free;
Some help of women God may send,
That Mary, full of grace, pleased may be.   Medieval miracle play

J OSEPH was an old man,
  An old man was he,
He married Virgin Mary,
The Queen of Galilee.

As Joseph and Mary was walkin',
Was walkin' one day,
"Here are apples, here are cherries,"
Mary did say.

Then Mary said to Joseph,
So meek and so mild,
"Joseph gather me some cherries,
For I am with child."

Then Joseph flew in anger,
In anger flew he,
"Let the father of the baby
Gather cherries for thee."

Jesus spoke a few words,
A few words spoke he,

"Give my mother some cherries,
Bow down, cherry tree!

"Bow down, cherry tree,
Low down to the ground."
Mary gathered cherries
And Joseph stood around.

Joseph took Mary
All on his right knee,
"What have I done, Lord?
Have mercy on me."

Then Joseph took Mary
All on his left knee,
"Oh, tell me, little baby,
when thy birth day will be."

"On the sixth day of January
My birth day will be,
When the stars in the elements
Will tremble with glee."

American version of
English carol

B LESSED Woman,
  Excellent Man,
Redeem for the dull the
Average Way,
That common ungifted
Natures may
Believe that their normal
Vision can
Walk to perfection.

W. H. Auden

V IGILATE animo,
in proximo est Dominus Deus noster.

Wide awake now!
The Lord God is so near!

Monastic liturgy

O sacred Lord of ancient Israel,
who showed yourself to Moses in the burning bush,
who gave him the holy law on Sinai mountain:
Come, stretch out your mighty hand to set us free.

Vespers antiphon

O come, O come, great Lord of might,
Who to your tribes on Sinai's height
In ancient times once gave the Law
In cloud and majesty and awe.

Latin hymn
Ninth century

I F the lost word is lost, if the spent word is spent
If the unheard, unspoken
Word is unspoken, unheard;
Still is the unspoken word, the Word unheard,
The Word without a word, the Word within
The world and for the world;
And the light shone in darkness and
Against the Word the unstilled world still whirled
About the centre of the silent Word.

T. S. Eliot

THE will of God be done by us,
The law of God be kept by us,
Our evil will controlled by us,
Our tongue in cheek be held by us,
Repentance timely made by us,
Christ's passion understood by us,
Each sinful crime be shunned by us,
Much on the *End* be mused by us,
And death be blessed found by us,
With angel's music heard by us,
And God's high praises sung by us,
Celtic hymn   For ever and for aye.

EARTH grown old, yet still so green,
Deep beneath her crust of cold
Nurses fire unfelt, unseen:
    Earth grown old.

We who live are quickly told:
Millions more lie hid between
    Inner swathings of her fold.

When will fire break up her screen?
    When will life burst thro' her mould?
Christina Rossetti   Earth, earth, earth, thy cold is keen,
Nineteenth century   Earth grown old.

I remember Grandfather blessing me: "May you see the Messiah put an end to exile and the reign of evil." A blessing that almost came true. It was night. I found myself transported into a strange and distant kingdom. In the shadow of the flames, the exiles were gathered. They came from everywhere, they spoke every language and told the same story. Seeing them together under the fiery sky, the child in me had thought: this is it; this is the end of time, the end of everything. Any moment the Messiah will appear out of the night, the Messiah of fear, the Messiah of death. I thought of my grandfather and I trembled for him, for myself. And for his blessing.   Elie Wiesel

O eternal God, the beginning and end, you who sustain all things, understand all things, who existed before all things, and who are without end, be with us, remain among us; strengthen our intentions, sanctify our souls and eradicate in us all that is evil. Enable us to make a good sacrifice and pour out your abundant blessings, and so enable us to enter into the holy of holies wherein dwells your presence.   Ethiopian liturgy

T WAS in the year that king Uzziah died,
    A vision by Isaiah espied:
A lofty throne, the Lord was set thereon;
And with his glory all the temple shone.
Bright seraphim were standing round about;
Six wings had every of that choir devout;
With twain he awesome veiled his face, and so
With twain he dreadful veiled his feet below,
With twain did he now hither, thither fly:
And thus aloud did one to another cry:

Holy is God, the Lord of Sabaoth,
Holy is God, the Lord of Sabaoth,
Holy is God, the Lord of Sabaoth,
Full of his glory are earth and heaven, both.
And at their cry the lintels moved apace,
And clouds of incense filled the Holy Place.   G. R. Woodward

THE LORD's messenger found Hagar by a spring in the wilderness, the spring on the road to Shur, and he asked, "Hagar, maid of Sarai, where have you come from and where are you going?" She answered, "I am running away from my mistress, Sarai." But the LORD's messenger told her: "Go back to your mistress and submit to her abusive treatment. I will make your descendants so numerous," added the LORD's messenger, "that they will be too many to count. Besides," the LORD's messenger said to her:

"You are now pregnant and shall bear a son;
  you shall name him Ishmael,
For the LORD has heard you,
  God has answered you.
He shall be a wild ass of a man,
  his hand against everyone,
  and everyone's hand against him;
In opposition to all his kin
  shall he encamp."

To the LORD who spoke to her she gave a name, saying, "You are the God of Vision"; she meant, "Have I really seen God and remained alive after my vision?" That is why the well is called Beer-lahai-roi. It is between Kadesh and Bered.

Genesis 16:7–16
A child is promised:
Ishmael

Hagar bore Abram a son, and Abram named the son whom Hagar bore him Ishmael. Abram was eighty-six years old when Hagar bore him Ishmael.

THE LORD appeared to Abraham by the terebinth of Mamre, as he sat in the entrance of his tent, while the day was growing hot. Looking up, he saw three men standing nearby. When he saw them, he ran from the entrance of the tent to greet them; and bowing to the ground, he said: "Sir, if I may ask you this favor, please do not go on past your servant. Let some water be brought, that you may bathe your feet, and then rest yourselves under the tree. Now that you have come this close to your servant, let me bring you a little food, that you may refresh yourselves; and afterward you may go on your way." "Very well," they replied, "do as you have said."

Abraham hastened into the tent and told Sarah, "Quick, three seahs of fine flour! Knead it and make rolls." He ran to the herd, picked out a tender, choice steer, and gave it to a servant, who quickly prepared it. Then he got some curds and milk, as well as the steer that had been prepared, and set these before them; and he waited on them under the tree while they ate.

"Where is your wife Sarah?" they asked him. "There in the tent," he replied. One of them said, "I will surely return to you about this time next year, and Sarah will then have a son." Sarah was listening at the entrance of the tent, just behind him. Now Abraham and Sarah were old, advanced in years, and Sarah had stopped having her womanly periods. So Sarah laughed to herself and said, "Now that I am so withered and my husband is so old, am I still to have sexual pleasure?" But the LORD said to Abraham: "Why did Sarah laugh and say, 'Shall I really bear a child, old as I am?' Is anything too marvelous for the LORD to do? At the appointed time next year, I will return to you, and Sarah will have a son." Because she was afraid, Sarah dissembled, saying, "I didn't laugh." But he said, "Yes you did."

Genesis 18:1–15
A child is promised:
Isaac

T HERE was a certain man from Zorah, of the clan of the Danites, whose name was Manoah. His wife was barren and had borne no children. An angel of the LORD appeared to the woman and said to her, "Though you are barren and have had no children, yet you will conceive and bear a son. Now, then, be careful to take no wine or strong drink and to eat nothing unclean. As for the son you will conceive and bear, no razor shall touch his head, for this boy is to be consecrated to God from the womb. It is he who will begin the deliverance of Israel from the power of the Philistines."

The woman went and told her husband, "A man of God came to me; he had the appearance of an angel of God, terrible indeed. I did not ask him where he came from, nor did he tell me his name. But he said to me, 'You will be with child and will bear a son. So take neither wine nor strong drink, and eat nothing unclean. For the boy shall be consecrated to God from the womb, until the day of his death.'" Manoah then prayed to the LORD. "O Lord, I beseech you," he said, "may the man of God whom you sent, return to us to teach us what to do for the boy who will be born."

God heard the prayer of Manoah, and the angel of God came again to the woman as she was sitting in the field. Since her husband Manoah was not with her, the woman ran in haste and told her husband. "The man who came to me the other day has appeared to me," she said to him; so Manoah got up and followed his wife. When he reached the man, he said to him, "Are you the one who spoke to my wife?" "Yes," he answered. Then Manoah asked, "Now, when that which you say comes true, what are we expected to do for the boy?" The angel of the LORD answered Manoah, "Your wife is to abstain from all the things of which I spoke to her. She must not eat anything that comes from the vine, nor take wine or strong drink, nor eat anything unclean. Let her observe all that I have commanded her." Then Manoah said to the angel of the LORD, "Can we persuade you to stay, while we prepare a kid for you?" But the angel of the LORD answered Manoah, "Although you press me, I will not partake of your food. But if you will, you may offer a holocaust to the LORD." Not knowing that it was the angel of the LORD, Manoah said to him, "What is your name, that we may honor you when your words come true?" The angel of the LORD answered him, "Why do you ask my name, which is mysterious?" Then Manoah took the kid with a cereal offering and offered it on the rock to the LORD, whose works are mysteries. While Manoah and his wife were looking on, as the flame rose to the sky from the altar, the angel of the LORD ascended in the flame of the altar. When Manoah and his wife saw this, they fell prostrate to the ground.

Judges 13:3–20, 24
A child is promised:
Samson

The woman bore a son and named him Samson.

THERE was a certain man from Ramathaim, Elkanah by name, a Zuphite from the hill country of Ephraim. He was the son of Jeroham, son of Elihu, son of Tohu, son of Zuph, an Ephraimite. He had two wives, one named Hannah, the other Peninnah; Peninnah had children, but Hannah was childless.

This man regularly went on pilgrimage from his city to worship the LORD of hosts and to sacrifice to him at Shiloh, where the two sons of Eli, Hophni and Phinehas, were ministering as priests of the LORD. When the day came for Elkanah to offer sacrifice, he used to give a portion each to his wife Peninnah and to all her sons and daughters, but a double portion to Hannah because he loved her, though the LORD had made her barren. Her rival, to upset her, turned it into a constant reproach to her that the LORD had left her barren. This went on year after year; each time they made their pilgrimage to the sanctuary of the LORD, Peninnah would approach her, and Hannah would weep and refuse to eat. Her husband Elkanah used to ask her; "Hannah, why do you weep, and why do you refuse to eat? Why do you grieve? Am I not more to you than ten sons?"

Hannah rose after one such meal at Shiloh, and presented herself before the LORD; at the time, Eli the priest was sitting on a chair near the doorpost of the LORD's temple. In her bitterness she prayed to the LORD, weeping copiously, and she made a vow, promising; "O LORD of hosts, if you look with pity on the misery of your handmaid, if you remember me and do not forget me, if you give your handmaid a male child, I will give him to the LORD for as long as he lives; neither wine nor liquor shall he drink, and no razor shall ever touch his head." As she remained long at prayer before the LORD, Eli watched her mouth, for Hannah was praying silently; though her lips were moving, her voice could not be heard. Eli, thinking her drunk, said to her, "How long will you make a drunken show of yourself? Sober up from your wine!" "It isn't that, my lord," Hannah answered. "I am an unhappy woman. I have had neither wine nor liquor; I was only pouring out my troubles to the LORD. Do not think your handmaid a ne'er-do-well; my prayer has been prompted by my deep sorrow and misery." Eli said, "Go in peace, and may the God of Israel grant you what you have asked of him." She replied, "Think kindly of your maidservant," and left. She went to her quarters, ate and drank with her husband, and no longer appeared downcast. Early the next morning they worshiped before the LORD, and then returned to their home in Ramah.

When Elkanah had relations with his wife Hannah, the LORD remembered her. She conceived, and at the end of her term bore a son whom she called Samuel, since she had asked the LORD for him.

1 Samuel 1:1–20
A child is promised:
Samuel

In the days of Herod, King of Judea, there was a priest named Zechariah of the priestly division of Abijah; his wife was from the daughters of Aaron, and her name was Elizabeth. Both were righteous in the eyes of God, observing all the commandments and ordinances of the Lord blamelessly. But they had no child, because Elizabeth was barren and both were advanced in years. Once when he was serving as priest in his division's turn before God, according to the practice of the priestly service, he was chosen by lot to enter the sanctuary of the Lord to burn incense. Then, when the whole assembly of the people was praying outside at the hour of the incense offering, the angel of the Lord appeared to him, standing at the right of the altar of incense. Zechariah was troubled by what he saw, and fear came upon him. But the angel said to him, "Do not be afraid, Zechariah, because your prayer has been heard. Your wife Elizabeth will bear you a son, and you shall name him John. And you will have joy and gladness, and many will rejoice at his birth, for he will be great in the sight of the Lord. He will drink neither wine nor strong drink. He will be filled with the holy Spirit even from his mother's womb, and he will turn many of the children of Israel to the Lord their God. He will go before him in the spirit and power of Elijah to turn the hearts of fathers toward children and the disobedient to the understanding of the righteous, to prepare a people fit for the Lord." Then Zechariah said to the angel, "How shall I know this? For I am an old man, and my wife is advanced in years." And the angel said to him in reply, "I am Gabriel, who stand before God. I was sent to speak to you and to announce to you this good news. But now you will be speechless and unable to talk until the day these things take place, because you did not believe my words, which will be fulfilled at their proper time."

Meanwhile the people were waiting for Zechariah and were amazed that he stayed so long in the sanctuary. But when he came out, he was unable to speak to them, and they realized that he had seen a vision in the sanctuary. He was gesturing to them but remained mute. Then, when his days of ministry were completed, he went home. After this time his wife Elizabeth conceived, and she went into seclusion for five months, saying, "So has the Lord done for me at a time when he has seen fit to take away my disgrace before others."

Luke 1:5–25
A child is promised:
John

I N the sixth month, the angel Gabriel was sent from God to a town of Galilee called Nazareth, to a virgin betrothed to a man named Joseph, of the house of David, and the virgin's name was Mary. And coming to her, he said, "Hail, favored one! The Lord is with you." But she was greatly troubled at what was said and pondered what sort of greeting this might be. Then the angel said to her, "Do not be afraid, Mary, for you have found favor with God. Behold, you will conceive in your womb and bear a son, and you shall name him Jesus. He will be great and will be called Son of the Most High, and the Lord God will give him the throne of David his father, and he will rule over the house of Jacob forever, and of his kingdom there will be no end." But Mary said to the angel, "How can this be, since I have no relations with a man?" And the angel said to her in reply, "The holy Spirit will come upon you, and the power of the Most High will overshadow you. Therefore the child to be born will be called holy, the Son of God. And behold, Elizabeth, your relative, has also conceived a son in her old age, and this is the sixth month for her who was called barren; for nothing will be impossible

Luke 1:26–38
A child is promised:
Jesus
for God." Mary said, "Behold, I am the handmaid of the Lord. May it be done to me according to your word." Then the angel departed from her.

S ALVATION to all that will is nigh;
That All, which always is All everywhere,
Which cannot sin, and yet all sins must bear,
Which cannot die, yet cannot choose but die,
Lo, faithful virgin, yields Himself to lie
In prison, in thy womb; and though He there
Can take no sin, nor thou give, yet He will wear,
Taken from thence, flesh, which death's force may try.
Ere by the spheres time was created, thou
Wast in his mind, Who is thy Son, and Brother;
Whom thou conceiv'st, conceiv'd; yea thou art now
Thy Maker's maker, and thy Father's mother;
Thou hast light in dark; and shut'st in little room,
Immensity cloister'd in thy dear womb.

John Donne
Seventeenth century

THERE stood in heaven a linden tree,
But, tho' 'twas honey-laden,
All angels cried, "No bloom shall be
Like that of one fair maiden."

Sped Gabriel on winged feet,
And passed through bolted portals
In Nazareth, a maid to greet,
Blest o'er all other mortals.

"Hail Mary!" quoth the angel mild.
"Of womankind the fairest:
The Virgin aye shalt thou be styled,
A babe although thou bearest."

"So be it!" God's handmaiden cried,
　"According to thy telling."
Whereon the angel smartly hied
　Up homeward to his dwelling.

This tiding filled his friends with glee:
　'Twas pass'd from one to other,
That 'twas Mary, and none but she.
　And God would call her Mother.

Dutch carol

WHEN Gabriel had spoken in due measure and had
heard immediately the responses of the Virgin,
He flew away and came to his bright and gleaming abode;
Then, it is probable that the young woman summoned
　　Joseph to her
　And said, "Where were you, my wise husband?
　Why did you not guard my virginity?
　For a certain winged being has given me a bridegroom.
　He has hung his words
Like earrings of pearls on my ears.
　Look, see how he has beautified me,
　As he adorned me with what he said to me. Just so you
　　will say to me
　In a short time, holy one,
　'Hail, virgin wife.'"

When Joseph saw the maiden whom God had blessed
　as highly favored,
　He was struck with fear and amazement,
　and he thought to himself:
"Just what manner of woman is this?" he said, "For today

she does not seem to me as she did yesterday.
Both terrible and sweet does she appear
to me now, and it gives me pause.
I gaze upon burning heat in snow,
Paradise in a furnace,
I gaze upon a smoking hill, upon a divine flower with
    young freshness,
Upon an awesome throne, on a pitiable footstool
Of the All-Merciful One. I do not understand the woman
    whom I took.
How, then, shall I say to her:
'Hail, virgin wife'?"

Romanos
Sixth century

A new work is come on hand
   Through might and grace of God's son,
To save the lost of every land;
   For now is free that erst was bound,
We may well sing: alleluja!

For Gabriel began it was
   Bright as the sunshine through the glass,
Thus was the Christ conceived for us;
   O Mary, mother, full of grace,
Well now sings she: alleluja!

Now is fulfilled the prophecy
   Of David and of Jeremy,
And also of Isaiah;
   Sing thee, therefore, both loud and high,
Both loud and high: alleluja!

Alleluja, this sweetest song
   Out of a green branch is sprung,
God send us the life that lasteth long;
   Now joy and bliss be us among,
That thus do sing: alleluja!

English carol
Fifteenth century

NOVA, nova:
Ave fit ex Eva.

Gabriell of hygh degre,
He cam down from Trynyte,
From Nazareth to Galalye, Nova, nova!
    Nova, nova: Ave fit ex Eva.

He mete a maydyn in a place;
He kneled down afore her face;
He sayd, Hayle, Mary full of grace. Nova, nova!
    Nova, nova: Ave fit ex Eva.

When the maydyn herd tel of this,
She was ful sore abashed, ywys,
And wened that she had done amys; Nova, nova!
    Nova, nova: Ave fit ex Eva.

Then said the angell, Dred not thou;
For ye be conceyved with grete vertu
Whose name shall be called Jhësu. Nova, nova!
    Nova, nova: Ave fit ex Eva.

Then said the maydyn, Verily,
I am your servant right truly;
Ecce ancilla domini. Nova, nova!
    Nova, nova: Ave fit ex Eva.

English lyric
Fifteenth century

O Flower of Jesse's stem,
    you have been raised up as a sign for all peoples;
rulers stand silent in your presence;
the nations bow down in worship before you.
Come, let nothing keep you from coming to our aid.

Vespers antiphon

O come, O Rod of Jesse's stem,
From every foe deliver them
That trust your mighty power to save,
And give them victory o'er the grave.

Latin hymn
Ninth century

ADAM and Eve stood under a tree,
A sweet and comely sight to see
For they were fair as fair could be,
Adam and Eve beneath the tree.

And on the tree the branches grew
Adorned with leaves of tender hue,
And they were fair as fair could be,
And Adam and Eve stood under the tree.

And on the branch a beauteous flower
Budded and bloomed from hour to hour,
The flower that on the branches grew
Adorned with leaves of tender hue,
And it was fair as fair could be,
And Adam and Eve stood under the tree.

And in that flower a fruit of gold
Lay hidden within the petals' fold,
The petals of the beauteous flower
That budded and bloomed from hour to hour,
The flower that on the branches grew
Adorned with leaves of tender hue,
And it was fair as fair could be,
And Adam and Eve stood under the tree.

But Eve put forth her hand anon,
And bit that fruit unto the stone,

The strange, forbidden fruit of gold
That hid within the petals' fold,
The petals of the beauteous flower
That budded and bloomed from hour to hour,
The flower that on the branches grew
Adorned with leaves of tender hue,
And the tree withered down to the ground so bare,
And Adam and Eve stood naked there.

But when the stone had fallen to earth,
It brought another tree to birth,
That tall and stately grew anon,
The tree that sprang from that fruit stone,
The strange forbidden fruit of gold
That hid within the petals' fold,
The petals of the beauteous flower
That budded and bloomed from hour to hour,
The flower that on the branches grew
Adorned with leaves of tender hue,
And it was fair as fair could be,
And Adam and Eve stood under the tree.

Dorothy L. Sayers

THE earth is your mother,
   she holds you.
The sky is your father,
he protects you.
Sleep,
sleep.
Rainbow is your sister,
she loves you.
The winds are your brothers,
they sing to you.
Sleep,

sleep.
We are together always.
We are together always.
There never was a time
when this
was not so.

Native American song

VANITY of vanities, the Preacher saith,
All things are vanity. The eye and ear
Cannot be filled with what they see and hear.
Like early dew, or like the sudden breath
Of wind, or like the grass that withereth,
Is man, tossed to and fro by hope and fear:
So little joy hath he, so little cheer,
Till all things end in the long dust of death.
Today is still the same as yesterday,
Tomorrow also even as one of them;
And there is nothing new under the sun:
Until the ancient race of Time be run,
The old thorns shall grow out of the old stem,
And morning shall be cold and twilight grey.

Christina Rossetti
Nineteenth century

MARIA walks amid the thorn, Kyrieleison,
Maria walks amid the thorn,
Which sev'n long years no leaf has born,
Jesus and Maria.

What 'neath her heart doth Mary bear, Kyrieleison,
A little child doth Mary bear,
Beneath her heart he nestles there,
Jesus and Maria.

And as the two were passing near, Kyrieleison,
Lo, roses on the thorn appear,
Lo, roses on the thorn appear,
Jesus and Maria.

Medieval German
carol

H AIL, O greenest branch,
sprung forth in the airy breezes
of the prayers of the saints.

So the time has come
that your sprays have flourished:
hail, hail to you,
because the heat of the sun has exuded from you
like the aroma of balm.

For the beautiful flower sprang from you
which gave all parched perfumes their aroma.

And they have radiated anew
in their full freshness.

Whence the skies bestowed dew upon the pasture,
and all the earth was made joyful
because her womb
brought forth corn
and because the birds of the firmament
built their nests in her.

Then there was a harvest ready for humankind
and a great rejoicing of banqueters,
whence, O sweet Virgin,
no joy is lacking in you.

Hildegard of Bingen
Twelfth century

EVE speaks:
 "Be fully reassured, my husband, by the words
    of your wife;
 For you will not find me again giving you bitter advice.
The ancient things have passed away,
    And Christ, the son of Mary, brings to light
      all things new.
Catch the scent of this fresh smell, and at once
      burst into new life.
    Stand erect like an ear of corn, for spring
      has overtaken you.
Jesus Christ breathes forth a fresh breeze.
    Escaping from the burning heat where you were,
Come, follow me to Mary and with me cling to
    Her immaculate feet, and she will at once
      be moved to pity,
      Mary, full of grace."

Adam speaks:
"I recognize, wife, the spring, and I sense the luxury
    Which we enjoyed in the past; for indeed I see
A new, another paradise, the virgin,
    Bearing in her arms the tree of life itself, which once
The Cherubim kept sacred, kept me from touching.
    And I, watching the untouched tree grow,
Am aware, wife, of a new breath-bringing life
    To me, who was formerly dust and lifeless clay,
Making me come alive. And now, strengthened
      by this fragrance,
Romanos   I advance to her who causes the fruit of our life to grow,
Sixth century   Mary, full of grace."

L O, how a Rose e'er blooming
From tender stem hath sprung!
Of Jesse's lineage coming
As seers of old have sung.
It came, a blossom bright,
Amid the cold of winter,
When half spent was the night.

O Flower, whose fragrance tender
With sweetness fills the air,
Dispel in glorious splendor
The darkness ev'rywhere;
Like us, yet very God,
From sin and death now save us,   German carol
And share our ev'ry load.   Fifteenth century

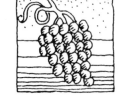

R EGARDING the eucharist, give thanks as follows:
First, concerning the cup:
"We give you thanks, our Father,
for the holy vine of David your servant,
which you have made known to us
through Jesus, your servant.
To you be glory for evermore."

Next, concerning the broken bread:
"We give you thanks, our Father,
for the life and knowledge
which you have made known to us
through Jesus, your servant.
To you be glory for evermore.
As this broken bread was scattered over the hills
and then, when gathered, became one,
so may the church be gathered

from the ends of the earth into your kingdom.
For yours is the glory and the power
through Jesus Christ for evermore."

The Didache
Second century

T HE days are coming, says the LORD, when I will fulfill the
promise I made to the house of Israel and Judah. In those
days, in that time, I will raise up for David a just shoot; he
shall do what is right and just in the land. In those days Judah
shall be safe and Jerusalem shall dwell secure; this is what
they shall call her: "The LORD our justice."

Jeremiah 33:14–16

E GREDIETUR virga de radice Jesse,
et replebitur omnis terra gloria Domini:
et videbit omnis caro salutare Dei.

A new shoot shall spring from the root of Jesse,
and all the earth will be filled with the glory of the Lord.
All flesh will see the salvation by our God.

Monastic liturgy

S INCE Adam, being free to choose,
Chose to imagine he was free
To choose his own necessity,
Lost in his freedom, Man pursues
The shadow of his images:
Today the Unknown seeks the known;
What I am willed to ask, your own
Will has to answer; child, it lies
Within your power of choosing to
Conceive the Child who chooses you.

W. H. Auden

EARFUL Adam and his sorrowing family begs this of you, O loving Virgin, in their exile from Paradise. Abraham begs it, David begs it. This is what the whole earth waits for, prostrate at your feet. It is right in doing so, for on your word depends comfort for the wretched, ransom for the captive, freedom for the condemned, indeed salvation for all the children of Adam, the whole of your race.

Answer quickly, O Virgin. Reply in haste to the angel, or rather through the angel to the Lord. Answer with a word, receive the word of God. Speak your own word, conceive the divine word. Breathe a passing word, embrace the eternal word.

Why do you delay, why are you afraid? Believe, give praise, and receive. Let humility be bold, let modesty be confident. Open your heart to faith, O blessed Virgin, your lips to praise, your womb to the Creator. See, the desired of all nations is at your door, knocking to enter. If he should pass by because of your delay, in sorrow you would begin to seek him afresh, the one whom your soul loves. Arise, hasten, open. Arise in faith, hasten in devotion, open in praise and thanksgiving. Behold, the handmaid of the Lord, she says, be it done to me according to your word.

Bernard
Twelfth century

WE do not pray that your birth according to the flesh shall be renewed as it once occurred upon this day. Rather do we pray that your invisible Godhead may be grafted into us. May that which was then accorded after the flesh to Mary alone now be granted in the spirit to the church: that faith unquestioning may conceive you, the spirit free of all corruption may bear you, the soul over-shadowed by the power of the Most High may quicken with you evermore. Go not forth from us; spring forth rather from within us.

Mozarabic rite

H AIL! by whom true hap has dawned.
Hail! by whom mishap has waned.
Hail! sinful Adam's recalling.
Hail! Eve's tears redeeming.
Hail! height untrodden by thought of people.
Hail! depth unscanned by angels' ken.
Hail! for the kingly throne thou art.
Hail! for who beareth all thou bearest?
Hail! O star that bore the Sun.
Hail! the womb of God enfleshed.
Hail! through whom things made are all new made.
Hail! through whom becomes a babe their maker.
Hail! through whom the maker is adored.
Orthodox liturgy   Hail! Bride unbrided.

T HERE came to my assistance,
Mary fair and bride:
As Anna bore Mary,
As Mary bore Christ,
As Eile bore John the Baptist
Without flaw in him,
Aid thou me in my unbearing,
    Aid me, O Bride!

As Christ was conceived of Mary
Full perfect on every hand,
Assist thou me, foster-mother,
The conception to bring from the bone,
And as thou didst aid the virgin of joy,
Without gold, without corn, without kine,
Aid thou me, great is my sickness,
Gaelic prayer   Aid me, O Bride!

THE three-fold terror of love; a fallen flare
Through the hollow of an ear;
Wings beating about the room;
The terror of all terrors that I bore
The Heavens in my womb.

Had I not found content among the shows
Every common woman knows,
Chimney corner, garden walk,
Or rocky cistern where we tread the clothes
And gather all the talk?

What is this flesh I purchased with my pains,
This fallen star my milk sustains,
This love that makes my heart's blood stop
Or strikes a sudden chill into my bones
And bids my hair stand up?

William Butler Yeats

O Key of David, O royal power of Israel,
controlling at your will the gate of heaven:
Come, break down the prison walls of death
for those who dwell in darkness and the shadow of death,
and lead your captive people into freedom.

Vespers antiphon

O come, O Key of David, come,
And open wide our heavenly home;
Make safe the way that leads on high,
And close the path to misery.

Latin hymn
Ninth century

BLESS earth with thine advent,   O Savior Christ!
And the golden gates   which in days gone by
Full long stood locked,   high Lord of heaven,
Bid thou swing open   and seek us out,
Humbly descending thyself   to earth.

We have need of thy mercy.   The dark death-shadow,
The accursed wolf,   has scattered thy sheep
And widely dispersed them;   what thou, O Lord,
Bought with thy blood, and   that doth the wicked one
Take into bondage,   and smiteth sore
Against our desire.   O Savior Lord,
In our inmost thoughts   we eagerly beg:
Hasten to help us,   miserable sinners,
That the prince of torment   may plunge to hell;
And thy handiwork   mount up on high,
Creator of humankind,   and come to righteousness.

Medieval English lyric

GOOD news; but if you ask me what it is, I know not;
It is a track of feet in the snow,
It is a lantern showing a path,
It is a door set open.

G. K. Chesterton

THE Word of God was made human in order that we
might be made divine. The Word displayed itself
through a body, that we might receive knowledge of the
invisible Father.

Athanasius
Fourth century

THREE old men, of whom one had a bad reputation, came one day to Abba Achilles. The first asked him, "Father make me a fishing net." "I will not make you one," he replied. Then the second one said, "Of your charity make one, so that we may have a souvenir of you in the monastery." But he said, "I do not have time." Then the third one, who had a bad reputation, said, "Make me a fishing net, so that I may have something from your hands, Father." Abba Achilles answered him at once, "For you, I will make one." Then the two other old men asked him privately, "Why did you not want to do what we asked you, but you promised to do what he asked?" The old man gave them this answer, "I told you I would not make one, and you were not disappointed, since you thought I had no time. But if I had not made one for him, he would have said, 'The old man has heard about my sin, and that is why he does not want to make me anything,' and so our relationship would have broken down. But now I have cheered his soul, so that he will not be overcome with grief."

The Sayings of the Desert Fathers

THE justice of God,
which will pass judgment on human justice,
will reveal itself with the brightness of sunshine
on the day of the resurrection,
but not right now.
Now Jesus must drink the chalice of suffering
    down to the last drop.
He must walk the way of the cross to the very end,
enduring the limitless atrocities of injustice
    against the innocent.

Leonardo Boff

HARK! my lover—here he comes
springing across the mountains,
  leaping across the hills.
My lover is like a gazelle
  or a young stag.

Here he stands behind our wall,
  gazing through the windows,
  peering through the lattices.
My lover speaks; he says to me,
  "Arise, my beloved, my beautiful one,
  and come!

"For see, the winter is past,
  the rains are over and gone.
The flowers appear on the earth,
  the time of pruning the vines has come,
  and the song of the dove is heard in our land.
The fig tree puts forth its figs,
  and the vines, in bloom, give forth fragrance.
Arise, my beloved, my beautiful one,
  and come!

"O my dove in the clefts of the rock,
  in the secret recesses of the cliff,
Let me see you,
  let me hear your voice,
For your voice is sweet,

Song of Songs 2:8–14   and you are lovely."

M ARY set out, proceeding in haste into the hill country to a town of Judah, where she entered Zechariah's house and greeted Elizabeth. When Elizabeth heard Mary's greeting, the baby stirred in her womb. Elizabeth was filled with the Holy Spirit, and cried out in a loud voice: "Blessed are you among women and blessed is the fruit of your womb. But who am I that the mother of my Lord should come to me? The moment your greeting sounded in my ears, the baby stirred in my womb for joy. Blessed is she who trusted that the Lord's words to her would be fulfilled."

Luke 1:39–45

YOU have trusted no town
With the news behind your eyes.
You have drowned Gabriel's word in thoughts like seas
And turned toward the stone mountain
To the treeless places.
Virgin of God, why are your clothes like sail?

Thomas Merton

THERE comes a ship a-sailing
With angels flying fast;
She bears a splendid cargo
  And has a mighty mast.

This ship is fully laden,
  Right to her highest board;
She bears the Son from heaven,
  God's high eternal word.

And that ship's name is Mary,
  Of flowers the rose is she,
And brings to us her baby
  From sin to set us free.

The ship made in this fashion,
  In which such store was cast,
Her sail is love's sweet passion,
  The Holy Ghost her mast.

German carol
Fifteenth century

HOW long, dear Savior, O how long
Shall this bright hour delay? Fly swifter round the
    wheel of time,
And bring the welcome day.

Jeremiah Ingalls
Eighteenth century

O radiant Dawn,
splendor of eternal light, sun of justice:
Come, shine on those who dwell in darkness
and the shadow of death.

Vespers antiphon

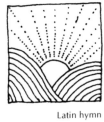

O come, O Dayspring from on high
And cheer us by your drawing nigh;
Disperse the gloomy clouds of night,
And death's dark shadow put to flight.

Latin hymn
Ninth century

A s the sun illumines not only the heaven and the whole
world, shining on both land and sea, but also sends rays
through windows and small chinks into the furthest recesses
of a house, so the Word, poured out everywhere, beholds
the smallest actions of our life.

Clement of Alexandria
Second century

E VERY part of this earth is sacred to my people. Every
shining pine needle, every sandy shore, every mist in the
dark woods, every clearing, every humming insect is holy in
the memory and experience of my people. The sap which
courses through the trees carries the memories of the red
people.

The white people's dead forget the country of their birth
when they go to walk among the stars. Our dead never forget
this beautiful earth for it is the mother of the red people. We
are part of the earth and it is part of us.

The perfumed flowers are our sisters; the deer, the horse, the
great eagle, these are our brothers. The rocky crests, the
juices of the meadows, the body heat of the pony, and

human beings—all belong to the same family.

For this land is sacred to us. This shining water that moves in the streams and rivers is not just water but the blood of our ancestors. If we sell you land, you must remember that it is sacred, and you must teach your children that it is sacred and that each ghostly reflection in the clear water of the lakes tells of events and memories in the life of my people. The water's murmur is the voice of my parent's parent.

The red people have always retreated before the advancing white people, as the mist of the mountains runs before the morning sun. But the ashes of our ancestors are sacred. Their graves are holy ground, and so these hills, these trees, this portion of the earth is consecrated to us.

You must teach your children that the ground between their feet is the ashes of our ancestors. So that they will respect the land, tell your children that the earth is rich with the lives of our kin. Teach your children what we have taught our children, that the earth is our mother. Whatever befalls the earth befalls the children of the earth.

This we know. The earth does not belong to us; we belong to the earth. This we know. All things are connected like the blood which unites one family. All things are connected. Whatever befalls the earth befalls the children of the earth. We do not weave the web of life, we are merely a strand in it. Whatever we do to the web, we do to ourselves.

Even the white people, whose God walks and talks with them as friend to friend, cannot be exempt from the common destiny. We may be brothers and sisters after all; we shall see. One thing we know, which the white people may one day discover—our God is the same God.

Anonymous

E VERYTHING beyond a certain distance is dark, and yet everything is full of being around us. This is the darkness, heavy with promises and threats, which the Christian will have to illuminate and animate with the divine presence.

Pierre Teilhard de Chardin

Do not make any judgment before the appointed time, until the Lord comes, for [the Lord] will bring to light what is hidden in darkness and will manifest the motives of our hearts, and then everyone will receive praise from God.

1 Corinthians 4:5

O what a beautiful city,
O what a beautiful city,
O what a beautiful city,
Twelve gates to the city, Hallelu!

Three gates in the east,
Three gates in the west,
Three gates in the north,
And three gates in the south,
Making twelve gates to the city, Hallelu!

American spiritual

By virtue of the creation and, still more, of the incarnation, nothing here below is profane for those who know how to see.

Pierre Teilhard
de Chardin

The King shall come when morning dawns
And light triumphant breaks;
When beauty gilds the eastern hills
And life to joy awakes.

Not, as of old, a little child
To suffer and to die,
But crowned with glory like the sun
That lights the morning sky.

The King shall come when morning dawns
And earth's dark night is past;
O haste the rising of that morn
Whose day shall ever last.

And let the endless bliss begin,
By weary saints foretold,
When right shall triumph over wrong,
And truth shall be extolled.

The King shall come when morning dawns
And light and beauty brings:
Hail, Christ the Lord! Your people pray:
Come quickly, King of kings.

John Brownlie
Nineteenth century

O RIETUR sicut sol Salvator mundi:
et descendet in uterum Virginis,
sicut imber super gramen, alleluia.

Like the sun shall the world's Savior rise
and the Lord shall come down to the virgin's womb
like gentle rain upon the grass. Alleluia.

Monastic liturgy

P RE-CHRISTIAN peoples who lived far north and who
suffered the archetypal loss of life and light with the
disappearance of the sun had a way of wooing back life and
hope. Primitives do not separate the natural phenomena
from their religious or mystical yearning, so nature and
mystery remained combined. As the days grew shorter and
colder and the sun threatened to abandon the earth, these
ancient people suffered the sort of guilt and separation
anxiety which we also know. Their solution was to bring all
ordinary action and daily routine to a halt. They gave in to
the nature of winter, came away from their fields and put
away their tools. They removed the wheels from their carts
and wagons, festooned them with greens and lights and

brought them indoors to hang in their halls. They brought the wheels indoors as a sign of a different time, a time to stop and turn inward. They engaged the feelings of cold and fear and loss. Slowly, slowly they wooed the sun-god back. And light followed darkness. Morning came earlier. The festivals announced the return of hope after primal darkness.

This kind of success—hauling the very sun back: the recovery of hope—can only be accomplished when we have had the courage to stop and wait and engage fully in the winter of our dark longing. Perhaps the symbolic energy of those wheels made sacred has escaped us and we wish to relegate our Advent wreaths to the realm of quaint custom or pretty decoration. Symbolism, however, has the power to put us directly in touch with a force or an idea by means of an image or an object—a "thing" can do that for us. The symbolic action bridges the gulf between knowing and believing. It integrates mind and heart. As we go about the process of clipping our greens and winding them on a hoop, we use our hands, we smell the pungent smell that fills the room, we think about our action. Our imagination is stirred.

Imagine what would happen if we were to understand that ancient prescription for this season literally and remove— just one—say just the right front tire from our automobiles and use this for our Advent wreath. Indeed, things would stop. Our daily routines would come to a halt and we would have the leisure to incubate. We could attend to our precarious pregnancy and look after ourselves. Having to stay put, we would lose the opportunity to escape or deny our feelings or becomings because our cars could not bring us away to the circus in town.

Gertrud Mueller
Nelson

R ENOUNCING henceforth all thoughts of looking back, and joyful with infinite gratitude, never fear to precede the dawn: to praise and bless and sing Christ your Lord.

Rule of Taizé

HANNAH worshiped the LORD. She said:
    My heart exults in the LORD,
my horn is exalted in my God.
I have swallowed up my enemies;
    I rejoice in my victory.
There is no Holy One like the LORD;
    there is no Rock like our God.

Speak boastfully no longer,
    nor let arrogance issue from your mouths.
For an all-knowing God is the LORD,
    a God who judges deeds.
The bows of the mighty are broken,
    while the tottering gird on strength.
The well-fed hire themselves out for bread,
    while the hungry fatten on spoil.
The barren wife bears seven sons,
    while the mother of many languishes.

The LORD puts to death and gives life,
    casts down to the nether world
    and raises up again.
The LORD makes poor and makes rich,
    humbles, and also exalts.
[The Lord] raises the needy from the dust;
    from the ash heap lifts up the poor,
To seat them with nobles
    and make a glorious throne their heritage.   1 Samuel 2:1–8

MARY said:
    My soul magnifies the Lord,
and my spirit rejoices in God my Savior
who has looked with favor on me, a lowly serving maid.
From this day all generations will call me blessed.

The Mighty One has done great things for me:
holy the name of the Lord,
whose mercy is on the God-fearing
from generation to generation.
The arm of the Lord is filled with strength,
scattering the proudhearted.
God cast the mighty from their thrones,
lifting up the lowly.
God filled the hungry with good things,
sending the rich away empty.

God has come to the help of Israel, the Lord's servant,
remembering mercy,
the mercy promised to our forebears,
Luke 1:46–55   to Abraham and his children for ever.

S ING we a song of high revolt;
Make great the Lord, God's name exalt:
Sing we the words of Mary's song
Of God at war with human wrong.

Sing we of God who deeply cares
And still with us our burden shares;
God, who with strength the proud disowns,
Brings down the mighty from their thrones.

By God the poor are lifted up;
God satisfies with bread and cup
The hungry folk of many lands:
The rich are left with empty hands.

God calls us to revolt and fight,
To seek for what is just and right.
To sing and live *Magnificat*
Fred Kaan   To ease all people's sorry lot.

O Ruler of all the nations,
the only joy of every human heart,
O Keystone of the mighty arch of humankind:
Come and save the creature you fashioned from the dust.

Vespers antiphon

O come, Desire of nations, bind
In one the hearts of humankind;
O bid our sad divisions cease,
And be for us our king of peace.

Latin hymn
Ninth century

W E who mystically represent the cherubim, singing the hymn "Thrice Holy" to the life-giving Trinity, let us now lay by all earthly cares, that we may receive the king of all things who comes amid unseen armies of angels. Alleluia. Alleluia. Alleluia.

Orthodox liturgy

I T is our clear duty to spare no effort in order to work for the moment when all war will be completely outlawed by international agreement. This goal, of course, requires the establishment of a universally acknowledged public authority vested with the effective power to ensure security for all, regard for justice, and respect for law. But before this desirable authority can be constituted, it is necessary for existing international bodies to devote themselves resolutely to the exploration of better means for obtaining common security.

If peace is to be established, the first condition is to root out the causes of discord among people which lead to wars — in the first place, injustice. Not a few of these causes arise out of excessive economic inequalities and out of hesitation to undertake necessary correctives. Some are due to the desire for power and to contempt for people, and at a deeper level, to envy, distrust, pride, and other selfish passions. Humanity cannot put up with such an amount of disorder; the result is that, even when war is absent, the world is constantly beset by strife and violence among people. Since the same evils are also to be found in the relations between nations, it is of the utmost importance, if these evils are to be overcome or forestalled and if headlong violence is to be curbed, for international bodies to work more effectively and more resolutely together and to coordinate their efforts. And finally, all should work unsparingly towards the creation of bodies designed to promote the cause of peace.

Vatican II
The Church in the
Modern World

ECCE veniet Dominus princeps regum terrae;
beati qui parati sunt occurrere illi.

See! The Ruler of all rulers will come.
Happy are all those who are ready now
to run out to the Lord.

Monastic liturgy

AT the center of the endeavors of the coming culture will loom this problem of power. The solution of it will remain crucial. Every decision faced by the future age— those determining the welfare or misery of humanity and those determining the life or death of humankind itself— will be decisions centered upon the problem of power. Although it will increase automatically as time moves on, the concern will not be its increase but first the restraint and then the proper use of power.

Romano Guardini

THOU art the wall-stone. . . . It befits thee well
   That thou shouldest be head of the great hall,
Locking together the long walls,
The flint unbroken in firm embrace,
That ever on earth the eyes of all
May look with wonder on the Lord of glory.
With cunning skill display thy craft
Triumphant, righteous, and quickly raise
Wall against wall. The work has need
That the craftsman come, the King himself;
That he then rebuild what now is broken,
The house under roof. He wrought the body,
The limbs of clay; now the Lord of life
From their foes must rescue this wretched host,
The woeful from dread, as he oft has done.

Medieval English lyric

CONSURGE, consurge: induere fortitudinem,
   brachium Domini.

Wake up, Lord! Rise up! Clothe yourself in strength!

Monastic liturgy

I begin through the grass once again to be bound
   to the Lord;
I can see, through a face that has faded, the face full of rest
Of the earth, of the mother, my heart with her heart
      in accord,
As I lie 'mid the cool green tresses that mantle her breast
I begin with the grass once again to be bound to the Lord.

By the hand of a child I am led to the throne of the King
   For a touch that now fevers me not is forgotten and far,
And His infinite sceptred hands that sway us can bring

Me in dreams from the laugh of a child to the song
of a star,
George William
Russell (AE)
On the laugh of a child I am borne to the joy of the King.

D OMINUS veniet, occurrite illi, dicentes:
Magnum principium, et regni ejus non erit finis:
Deus, fortis, dominator, princeps pacis, alleluia.

The Lord is coming, run out then shouting:
Greatest of all, rule forever!
Monastic liturgy
Our strong God, our prince of peace, alleluia!

Z ECHARIAH, the father of John, filled with the Holy Spirit,
uttered this prophecy:

Blessed are you, O Lord, the God of Israel!
You have come to your people and set them free.
You have raised up for us a horn of deliverance
in the house of your servant David.
Through the mouth of your holy prophets of old
you promised liberation from our enemies,
from the hands of all who hate us.

You promised to show mercy to our forebears
and to remember your holy covenant.
This was the oath you swore to our father Abraham:
that, rescued from the hands of our enemies,
we are free to worship you without fear,
holy and righteous in your sight
all the days of our life.

You, my child, shall be called the prophet
of the Most High,

for you will go before the Lord to prepare the way,
to give God's people knowledge of salvation
    by the forgiveness of their sins.
In the tender compassion of our God
the morning sun will break upon us,
to shine on those who dwell in darkness
    and the shadow of death,
and to guide our feet in the way of peace.

                                           Luke 1:68–79

V ENI Domine visitare nos in pace,
  ut laetemur coram te corde perfecto.

Come and visit us in peace, Lord,
and we will rejoice with hearts renewed.

                               Monastic liturgy

C HRIST climbed down
  from his bare Tree
this year
and ran away to where
there were no rootless Christmas trees
hung with candycanes and breakable stars

Christ climbed down
from his bare Tree
this year
and ran away to where
there were no gilded Christmas trees
and no tinsel Christmas trees
and no tinfoil Christmas trees
and no pink plastic Christmas trees
and no gold Christmas trees

and no black Christmas trees
and no powderblue Christmas trees
hung with electric candles
and encircled by tin electric trains
and clever cornball relatives

Christ climbed down
from his bare Tree
this year
and ran away to where
no intrepid Bible salesmen
covered the territory
in two-tone cadillacs
and where no Sears Roebuck creches
complete with plastic babe in manger
arrived by parcel post
the babe by special delivery
and where no televisioned Wise Men
praised the Lord Calvert Whiskey

Christ climbed down
from his bare Tree
this year
and ran away to where
no fat handshaking stranger
in a red flannel suit
and a fake white beard
went around passing himself off
as some sort of North Pole saint
crossing the desert to Bethlehem
Pennsylvania
in a Volkswagen sled
drawn by rollicking Adirondack reindeer
with German names
and bearing sacks of Humble Gifts
from Saks Fifth Avenue
for everybody's imagined Christ child

Christ climbed down
from his bare Tree
this year
and ran away to where
no Bing Crosby carolers
groaned of a tight Christmas
and where no Radio City angels
iceskated wingless
thru a winter wonderland
into a jinglebell heaven
daily at 8:30
with Midnight Mass matinees

Christ climbed down
from his bare Tree
this year
and softly stole away into
some anonymous soul
He waits again
an unimaginable
and impossibly
Immaculate Reconception
the very craziest
of Second Comings

Lawrence Ferlinghetti

To speak of Jesus as the Compassion of God allows for human initiative in Jesus in every phase of a redemptive incarnation without any denial of divine initiative. It allows for the progressive human identification with the redemptive initiative of God so that Jesus becomes wholly one with the divine compassion and therefore becomes truly divine without contradiction either of the unity and transcendence of God or of the authentic humanity of Jesus.

Monika Hellwig

Vespers antiphon

O Emmanuel, ruler and lawgiver,
  desire of the nations,
savior of all people:
Come and set us free, Lord our God.

O come, O come, Emmanuel,
  And ransom captive Israel,
That mourns in lonely exile here
Until the Son of God appear.

Latin hymn
Ninth century

THEREFORE the Lord himself will give you this sign: the
  virgin shall be with child, and bear a son, and shall
name him Emmanuel.

Isaiah 7:14

KNOW, O people, and be appalled!
  Give ear, all you distant lands!
  Arm, but be crushed! Arm, but be crushed!
Form a plan, and it shall be thwarted;
  make a resolve, and it shall not be carried out,
  for "With us is God!"

Isaiah 8:9–10

IT is both terrible and comforting to dwell in the inconceiv-
  able nearness of God, and so to be loved by God that the
first and last gift is infinity and inconceivability itself. But we
have no choice. God is with us.

Karl Rahner

O N that day it shall be said to Jerusalem:
"Do not fear, O Zion;
let not your hands grow weak.
The LORD, your God, is in your midst,
  a mighty one who gives victory;
the LORD will rejoice over you with gladness,
  and will renew you in love;
the LORD will exult over you with loud singing
  as on a day of festival."

Zephaniah 3:16–18

N O one can celebrate a genuine Christmas without
being truly poor. The self-sufficient, the proud, those
who, because they have everything, look down on others,
those who have no need even of God—for them there will
be no Christmas. Only the poor, the hungry, those who need
someone to come on their behalf, will have that someone.
That someone is God, Emmanuel, God-with-us. Without
poverty of spirit there can be no abundance of God.

Oscar Romero

T HE church asks us to understand that Christ, who came
once in flesh, is prepared to come again. When we
remove all obstacles to his presence he will come, at any
hour and moment, to dwell spiritually in our hearts, bringing
with him the riches of his grace.

Charles Borromeo
Sixteenth century

T HE very Son of God, older than the ages, the invisible,
the incomprehensible, the incorporeal, the beginning
of beginning, the light of light, the fountain of life and
immortality, the image of the archetype, the immovable
seal, the perfect likeness, the definition and word of the

Gregory Nazianzen
Fourth century

Father: He it is who comes to his own image and takes our nature for the good of our nature and unites himself to an intelligent soul for the good of my soul, to purify like by like.

Gerard Manley
Hopkins
Nineteenth century

IN a flash, at a trumpet crash,
I am all at once what Christ is, since he was what I am.

CRASTINA die delebitur iniquitas terrae:
et regnabit super nos Salvator mundi.

Tomorrow the sins of the world will be taken away
and the Savior will rule over us.

Monastic liturgy

TO cleave to God hidden beneath the inward and outward forces which animate our being and sustain it in its development is ultimately to open ourselves to, and put trust in, all the breaths of life.

Pierre Teilhard
de Chardin

CHRISTMAS Eve is the feast day of our first parents, Adam and Eve. They are commemorated as saints in the calendars of the Eastern churches (Greeks, Syrians, Copts). Under the influence of this Oriental practice, their veneration spread also to the West and became very popular toward the end of the first millennium of the Christian era. The Latin church has never officially introduced their feast, though it did not prohibit their popular veneration. In many old churches of Europe their statues may still be seen among the images of the saints. Boys and girls who bore the names of Adam and Eve (quite popular in past centuries) celebrated their "Name Day" with great rejoicing. In Germany the custom began in the sixteenth century of putting up a "paradise tree" in the homes to honor the first parents. This was a fir tree laden with apples, and from it developed the modern Christmas tree.

Francis X. Weiser

THE Lord at first did Adam make
Out of the dust and clay,
And in his nostrils breathed life,
E'en as the scriptures say.
And then in Eden's Paradise
He placed him to dwell,
That he within it should remain,
To dress and keep it well.

Now let good Christians all begin
An holy life to live,
And to rejoice and merry be,
For this is Christmas Eve.

Now mark the goodness of the Lord
Which he for mankind bore;
His mercy soon he did extend,
Lost man for to restore:
And then, for to redeem our souls
From death and hellish thrall,
He said his own dear Son should be
The Savior of us all.

Now for the blessings we enjoy,
Which are from heaven above,
Let us renounce all wickedness
And live in perfect love:
Then shall we do Christ's own command,

E'en his own written word;
And when we die, in heaven shall
Enjoy our living Lord.

And now the tide is nigh at hand,
In which our Savior came;
Let us rejoice and merry be
In keeping of the same:
Let's feed the poor and hungry souls,
And such as do it crave;
Then when we die, in heaven we
English carol   Our sure reward shall have.

FAREWELE, Advent; Christmas is cum;
Farewele fro us both alle and sume.

With paciens thou hast us fedde
And made us go hungrie to bedde;
For lak of mete we were nyghe dedde;
Farewele fro us both alle and sume.

While thou haste be within oure howse
We ete no puddynges ne no sowce,
But stynking fisshe not worth a lowce;
Farewele fro us both alle and sume.

There was no fresshe fisshe ferre ne nere;
Salt fisshe and samon was to dere,
And thus we have had hevy chere;
Farewele fro us both alle and sume.

Oure brede was browne, oure ale was thynne,
Oure brede was musty in the bynne,

Oure ale soure or we did begynne;
Farewele fro us both alle and sume.

The tyme of Cristes feest natall
We will be mery, grete and small,
And thou shalt goo oute of this halle;
Farewele fro us both alle and sume.

English carol
Fifteenth century

O come, let us rejoice in the Lord, as we declare this present mystery: The partition wall of disunion has been destroyed, the flaming sword is turned back, and the Cherubim withdraw from the Tree of Life, and I partake of the food of Paradise, whence because of disobedience, I was expelled. For the image immutable of the Father, the image of eternity, takes the form of a servant, having come from a Mother unwedded, yet having suffered no change: for that which he was that he remains, being very God; and that which he was not he has assumed, becoming flesh because of his love toward humankind. Unto him let us cry aloud: O God, who was born a Virgin, have mercy upon us.

By the command of Caesar were the people inscribed; and we faithful have been inscribed with the name of the Godhead, of you, our God, who have become flesh. Great is your mercy. O Lord, glory to you.

Orthodox liturgy

JUDEA et Jerusalem, nolite timere:
cras egrediemini, et Dominus erit vobiscum, alleluia.

Judea and Jerusalem, do not be afraid:
Tomorrow you shall set out and the Lord will be with you.
Alleluia.

Monastic liturgy

HODIE scietis quia veniet Dominus;
et mane videbitis gloriam ejus.

Today you know that the Lord will come
and in the morning you shall see God's glory.

Monastic liturgy

SUDDEN as sweet
Come the expected feet.
All joy is young and new all art,
And he, too, whom we have by heart.

Alice Meynell

IT is strange that the gospel read at the beginning of the time of preparation for Christmas is that of the end of the whole history of the world. Yet that is not really surprising. For what is afoot in a small beginning is best recognized by the magnitude of its end. What was really meant and actually happened by the coming, the "advent," of the redeemer is best gathered from that completion of his coming which we rather misleadingly call the "second coming." For in reality it is the fulfillment of his *one* coming which is still in progress at the present time.

Karl Rahner

IN the last weeks [before Advent] the lofty theme of a "blessed hope" is highlighted. The autumn of the church year is devoted to preparation for the end of life and the second coming of Christ. Now we more readily see the truth: Advent is really a continuation of the church's autumn season, her preparation for the Savior's return. In this light Christmas and Epiphany are one great feast oriented to the parousia.

This is beautifully expressed in the epistle of the first Mass of Christmas: "Awaiting our blessed hope, that is, the glorious coming of the great God, our Savior Christ Jesus." "Awaiting our blessed hope," that is Advent; "the glorious coming of the great God" is Epiphany. Note that the Latin *adventus* corresponds to the Greek *epiphaneia*. The fulfillment of Advent, therefore, is Epiphany. Although Christmas is still predominantly historical, there is no mistaking Epiphany as a parousia feast, as "the glorious coming of the great God, our Savior Christ Jesus."

Pius Parsch

S INCE the coming of Christ goes on forever—he is always he who is to come in the world and in the church—there is always an Advent going on.

Jean Danielou

M ARANA tha.

1 Corinthians
16:22

Endnotes

The Approach of Advent

CREATOR OF THE STARS OF NIGHT

Creator of: From *The Hymnal 1982*, verses 1, 2, 4, 5. Copyright ©, Church Pension Fund. Used with permission.

For many: Chrysogonus Waddell, OCSO. *Liturgy*, vol. 22, no. 2, 1988. "Saint Bernard and the Advent Hymn *Conditor alme siderum*."

When the Man: From the *Revised Standard Version Bible*. Copyright © 1946, 1952, 1971 by the Division of Christian Education of the National Council of Churches of Christ in the U.S.A., as emended in the *Lectionary for the Christian People*, copyright © 1986, 1987, 1988 by Pueblo Publishing Company, Inc. Used with permission. All rights reserved.

THE APPROACH OF ADVENT

Advent is: From *Days of the Lord*, William G. Storey. Copyright © 1965, Herder and Herder. Reprinted by permission of The Crossroad Publishing Company.

"Adventus": From *The Dynamics of the Liturgy*, Hans A. Reinhold. Macmillan Publishing Company, 1961.

With inward pain: From *Kentucky Harmony*, part two, 1816.

Nobody knows: From *Christmas Every Christmas*, Hubert M. Dunphy, OFM. The Bruce Publishing Company, Milwaukee, 1960.

Our time: From *The Shaking of the Foundations*, Paul Tillich, Charles Scribner's Sons, a subsidiary of Macmillan Publishing Company, 1948.

Winter wakeneth: Can be found in *Oxford Book of Carols*, 1936.

Passing away: From *The Pre-Raphaelites and Their Circle*, Cecil Y. Lang, ed., University of Chicago Press, 1975.

Beloved: Excerpts from the English translation of *Liturgy of the Hours* © 1974, International Committee on English in the Liturgy, Inc. (ICEL). All rights reserved.

Love is: From "East Coker" in *Four Quartets*. Copyright © 1943, T. S. Eliot; renewed 1971, Esne Valerie Eliot. Reprinted by permission of Harcourt Brace Jovanovich, Inc.

Eternity is: From *The Complete Writings*, William Blake. Published by Oxford University Press, 1966.

How sour: *Richard II*, Act V, Scene 5.

Time, that: From *The Collected Poems of Sigfried Sassoon, 1908–1956*. Copyright © 1918, 1920, E. P. Dalton and Company; 1936, 1946, 1947, 1948, Sigfried Sassoon. All rights reserved. Reprinted by permission of Viking Penguin, Inc.

Advent is: From *The Prison Meditations of Father Delp*, Alfred Delp. Copyright © 1968, Herder and Herder. Reprinted by permission of The Crossroad Publishing Company.

Abba John: From *Desert Wisdom*, Yushi Nomura. Copyright © 1982, Yushi Nomura. Reprinted by permission of Doubleday, a division of Bantam, Doubleday, Dell Publishing Group, Inc.

The day after: From *Sir, We Would Like to See Jesus*, Walter J. Burghardt. Copyright © 1982, Paulist Press. Used with permission.

What happened: From *Second Coming*, Walker Percy. Published by Farrar, Straus & Giroux, Inc., 1980.

The reign of God: From *Passion of Christ, Passion of the World*, Leonardo Boff, Orbis Books, 1987. Used with permission.

As to the times: From the *Revised Standard Version Bible*. Copyright © 1946, 1952, 1971 by the Division of Christian Education of the National Council of Churches of Christ in the U.S.A., as emended in the *Lectionary for the Christian People*, copyright © 1986, 1987, 1988 by Pueblo Publishing Company, Inc. Used with permission. All rights reserved.

Abba Poemen: From *Desert Wisdom*, Yushi Nomura. Copyright © 1982, Yushi Nomura. Reprinted by permission of Doubleday, a division of Bantam, Doubleday, Dell Publishing Group, Inc.

Darkness provides: From *The Jesus Story, Our Life As Story in Christ*, John Navone. Copyright © 1979, The Order of St. Benedict, Inc. Published by The Liturgical Press, Collegeville, Minnesota. Used with permission.

Advent then: From *Living the Christian Seasons*, Charles K. Riepe. Copyright © 1964, Herder and Herder. Reprinted by permission of The Crossroad Publishing Company.

Come, and make: From the hymn "Come, Lord, and tarry not." Music can be found in *Worship*, #366.

To you, O Lord: From *The Psalms: A New Translation for Prayer and Worship*, Gary Chamberlain. Copyright © 1984, The Upper Room. Used by permission of the author. All rights reserved.

NOVEMBER 29: DOROTHY DAY

When we handle: From *Jesus, the Word to Be Spoken*, Mother Teresa of Calcutta, Servant Publishers, Ann Arbor, Michigan.

After 1976: From *Dorothy Day: A Biography*, William Miller. Copyright © 1982, William D. Miller. Reprinted by permission of Harper and Row Publishers.

Alice Paul: From "The Outrider" column, Garry Wills. Copyright © 1980, Universal Press Syndicate. Used with permission. All rights reserved.

A brother said: From *Desert Wisdom*, Yushi Nomura. Copyright © 1982, Yushi Nomura. Reprinted by permission of Doubleday, a division of Bantam, Doubleday, Dell Publishing Group, Inc.

In each of our lives: From *Jesus, the Word to Be Spoken*, Mother Teresa of Calcutta, Servant Publishers, Ann Arbor, Michigan.

This morning: From *The Dorothy Day Book*, Margaret Quigley and Michael Garvey, eds. Templegate Publishers, Springfield, Illinois, 1982.

I feel: From *The Dorothy Day Book*, Margaret Quigley and Michael Garvey, eds. Templegate Publishers, Springfield, Illinois, 1982.

NOVEMBER 30: ANDREW, APOSTLE

Andrew the apostle: From *Liturgical Readings: The Lessons of the Temporal Cycle and the Principal Feasts of the Sanctoral Cycle According to the Monastic Breviary*. Grail: St. Meinrad, Indiana, 1943. Reprinted with permission.

Blessed feasts: From *Keeping the Church Year*, H. Boone Porter, The Seabury Press, 1977.

DECEMBER 2: MARTYRS OF EL SALVADOR

Archbishop Romero: From *Memory of Fire: Volume III: Century of the Wind*, Eduardo Galeano, translated by Cedric Belfrage. Translation copyright © 1988, Cedric Belfrage. Reprinted by permission of Pantheon Books, a Division of Random House, Inc. Used with permission.

The First Week

THE FIRST WEEK: WATCH!

Take heed: From the *Revised Standard Version Bible*. Copyright © 1946, 1952, 1971 by the Division of Christian Education of the National Council of Churches of Christ in the U.S.A., as emended in the *Lectionary for the Christian People*, copyright © 1986, 1987, 1988 by Pueblo Publishing Company, Inc. Used with permission. All rights reserved.

You, O Lord: From the *Revised Standard Version Bible*. Copyright © 1946, 1952, 1971 by the Division of Christian Education of the National Council of Churches of Christ in the U.S.A., as emended in the *Lectionary for the Christian People*, copyright © 1986, 1987, 1988 by Pueblo Publishing Company, Inc. Used with permission. All rights reserved.

O Savior: Text copyright © 1978, *Lutheran Book of Worship*. Reprinted by permission of Augsburg Fortress.

Though the Lord: Excerpts from the English translation of *Liturgy of the Hours* © 1974, International Committee on English in the Liturgy, Inc. (ICEL). All rights reserved.

Return, O God: From *Kentucky Harmony*, part one, 1816.

There were some: From *Memory of Fire: Volume III: Century of the Wind*, Eduardo Galeano, translated by Cedric Belfrage. Translation copyright © 1988, Cedric Belfrage. Reprinted by permission of Pantheon Books, a Division of Random House, Inc. Used with permission.

Apocalypse is: From *The New Testament without Illusion*, John L. McKenzie. Copyright © 1982, John L. McKenzie. Reprinted by permission of The Crossroad Publishing Company.

THE FIRST WEEK: SOON AND VERY SOON

One of the: From *The Advent of God*, Johannes Baptist Metz, translated by John Drury, Newman Press, 1970.

O Israel: Copyright © 1963, Ladies of the Grail, England. Used with permission of GIA Publications, Chicago, Illinois, exclusive agent. All rights reserved.

Soon and very soon: Music can be found in *Lead Me, Guide Me*, #4. Copyright © 1976, Lexicon Music, Inc., Newbury Park, California.

THE FIRST WEEK: JERUSALEM, BE GLAD

Expectation—anxious: From *The Time of the Spirit, Readings through the Christian Year,* selected and edited by George Emery, Richard Harries and Kallistos Ware, 1984. Reprinted by permission of St. Vladimir's Seminary Press.

They watch: From *Parochial and Plain Sermons,* vol. 4, John Henry Cardinal Newman. Published by Longmans, Green and Co., Ltd.

We ask: From *The Time of the Spirit, Readings through the Christian Year,* selected and edited by George Emery, Richard Harries and Kallistos Ware, 1984. Reprinted by permission of St. Vladimir's Seminary Press.

What has straw: From the *Revised Standard Version Bible.* Copyright © 1946, 1952, 1971 by the Division of Christian Education of the National Council of Churches of Christ in the U.S.A., as emended in the *Lectionary for the Christian People,* copyright © 1986, 1987, 1988 by Pueblo Publishing Company, Inc. Used with permission. All rights reserved.

My Lord: Music can be found in *Lead Me, Guide Me,* #9.

THE FIRST WEEK: WAKE, O WAKE

The dominion: From the *Revised Standard Version Bible.* Copyright © 1946, 1952, 1971 by the Division of Christian Education of the National Council of Churches of Christ in the U.S.A., as emended in the *Lectionary for the Christian People,* copyright © 1986, 1987, 1988 by Pueblo Publishing Company, Inc. Used with permission. All rights reserved.

When the midnight cry: From *The Southern Harmony,* 1854.

Hear, you maidens: From the medieval miracle play *Sponsus (The Bridegroom).*

Wake, O wake: Text copyright © 1982, Hope Publishing Company, Carol Stream, Illinois. All rights reserved. Used with permission.

Awake, my soul: From *The Gift to Be Simple: Songs, Dances and Rituals of the American Shakers,* Edward D. Andrews. Published by Dover Publications, Inc., New York.

Night is: From *Markings,* Dag Hammarskjöld, translated by Leif Sjöberg and W. H. Auden. Translation copyright © 1964, Alfred A. Knopf, Inc. and

Faber and Faber, Ltd. Reprinted by permission of Alfred A. Knopf, Inc.

THE FIRST WEEK: THE DAY OF THE LORD

Above the clamor: Excerpts from the English translation and the original alternative opening prayers from *The Roman Missal* © 1973, International Committee on English in the Liturgy, Inc. (ICEL). All rights reserved.

Alone, alone: From *W. H. Auden: Collected Poems,* Edward Mendelson, ed. Copyright © 1944, renewed 1972 by W. H. Auden. Reprinted by permission of Random House, Inc.

We are: From *The Broken Body,* Jean Vanier, 1988. Reprinted by permission of Paulist Press and Darton Longman & Todd.

DECEMBER 6: NICHOLAS

O Shepherd: Copyright © 1963, Ladies of the Grail, England. Used with permission of GIA Publications, Chicago, Illinois, exclusive agent. All rights reserved.

St. Nicholas: From *The Church's Year of Grace,* Pius Parsch, translated by William G. Heidt, OSB. Copyright © 1959, The Order of St. Benedict, Inc. Published by The Liturgical Press, Collegeville, Minnesota. Used with permission.

The celebration: From *The Orthodox Faith,* vol. ii, Thomas Hopko. Copyright © 1972, Orthodox Church of America. Used with permission.

O you: From *The Winter Pascha,* Thomas Hopko, 1984. Reprinted by permission of St. Vladimir's Seminary Press.

A voyce: From *The Early English Carols,* published by Clarendon Press.

Children's Letters: From *Handbook of Christian Feasts and Customs,* Frances X. Weiser. Copyright © 1952, Society of Jesus of New England, Boston. Published by Harcourt Brace Jovanovich, Inc. Used with permission.

A desire: From *To Dance with God.* Copyright © 1986, Gertrud Mueller Nelson. Reprinted by permission of Paulist Press.

Our eyes: From the cantata "St. Nicolas," music by Benjamin Britten, text by Eric Crozier, 1948.

The Second Week

THE SECOND WEEK: THE WELCOME TABLE

There shall come: From the *Revised Standard Version Bible.* Copyright © 1946, 1952, 1971 by the Division of Christian Education of the National Council of Churches of Christ in the U.S.A., as emended in the *Lectionary for the Christian People,* copyright © 1986, 1987, 1988 by Pueblo Publishing Company, Inc. Used with permission. All rights reserved.

DECEMBER 8: THE IMMACULATE CONCEPTION

O Adam and Eve: From *The Winter Pascha,* Thomas Hopko, 1984. Reprinted by permission of St. Vladimir's Seminary Press.

The man and woman: From the *Revised Standard Version Bible.* Copyright © 1946, 1952, 1971 by the Division of Christian Education of the National Council of Churches of Christ in the U.S.A., as emended in the *Lectionary for the Christian People,* copyright © 1986, 1987, 1988 by Pueblo Publishing Company, Inc. Used with permission. All rights reserved.

The Theotokos: From *The Winter Pascha,* Thomas Hopko, 1984. Reprinted by permission of St. Vladimir's Seminary Press.

Of man's: From *Paradise Lost,* John Milton

Hail Mary: From *Eastern Christian Liturgies,* Peter D. Day. Published by Irish University Press, 1972.

Hail, O most worthy: From *An Anthology of Old English Poetry,* translated by Charles W. Kennedy. Published by Oxford University Press, 1960. Used with permission.

THE SECOND WEEK: A DRY AND WEARY LAND

O God: Copyright © 1963, Ladies of the Grail, England. Used with permission of GIA Publications, Chicago, Illinois, exclusive agent. All rights reserved.

Ask not: From *The Eternal Year,* Karl Rahner. Published by Helicon, Baltimore, Maryland, 1964.

I don't know: From a speech by Martin Luther King, Jr., given on August 28, 1963, Washington, D.C.

DECEMBER 10: THOMAS MERTON

The Advent mystery: From *Seasons of Celebration,* Thomas Merton. Published by Farrar, Straus & Giroux, 1965.

Merton's most: From *Merton: A Biography,* Monica Furlong. Copyright © 1980, Monica Furlong. Reprinted by permission of Harper and Row Publishers.

The sermon: From *Merton: By Those Who Knew Him Best,* Paul Wilkes, ed. Copyright © 1984, Paul Wilkes. Reprinted by permission of Harper and Row Publishers.

All of the branches: From *The Collected Poems of Thomas Merton.* Copyright © 1968, Abbey of Gethsemani, Inc. Copyright © 1977, Trustees of the Merton Legacy Trust. Reprinted by permission of New Directions Publishing Company.

Charm with: From *The Collected Poems of Thomas Merton.* Copyright © 1968, Abbey of Gethsemani, Inc.; copyright © 1977, Trustees of the Merton Legacy Trust. Reprinted by permission of New Directions Publishing Company.

THE SECOND WEEK: PLOWSHARES

Peace is more: From *Vatican Council II, The Conciliar and Post Conciliar Documents,* vol. 1, Austin Flannery, OP, ed. Published by Costello Publishing, Inc., Northport, New York. Used with permission.

Take off: From *The Jerusalem Bible,* copyright © 1966, Darton, Longman & Todd, Ltd. and Doubleday, a division of Bantam, Doubleday, Dell Publishing Group, Inc. Used with permission.

Father in heaven: Excerpts from the English translation and the original alternative opening prayers from *The Roman Missal* © 1973, International Committee on English in the Liturgy, Inc. (ICEL). All rights reserved.

DECEMBER 12: OUR LADY OF GUADALUPE

God saw: Excerpts from the English translation of *Liturgy of the Hours* © 1974, International Committee on English in the Liturgy, Inc. (ICEL). All rights reserved.

The joy: From *Vatican Council II, The Conciliar and Post Conciliar Documents,* vol. 1, Austin Flannery, OP, ed. Published by Costello Publishing, Inc., Northport, New York. Used with permission.

They've come: Text copyright © 1983, 1984 by Willard F. Jabusch.

THE SECOND WEEK: WEALTH OF THE POOR

In an age: From *A Contemporary Meditation on Hope,* John Heagle. Reprinted by permission of The

Thomas More Press, Chicago, Illinois.

With the drawing: From "East Coker" in *Four Quartets.* Copyright © 1943, T. S. Eliot; renewed 1971, Esne Valerie Eliot. Reprinted by permission of Harcourt Brace Jovanovich, Inc.

Rise up: Excerpts from the English translation of *Liturgy of the Hours* © 1974, International Committee on English in the Liturgy, Inc. (ICEL). All rights reserved.

Deliver us: Copyright © 1963, Ladies of the Grail, England. Used with permission of GIA Publications, Chicago, Illinois, exclusive agent. All rights reserved.

The Uruguayan: From *Memory of Fire: Volume III: Century of the Wind,* Eduardo Galeano, translated by Cedric Belfrage. Translation copyright © 1988, Cedric Belfrage. Reprinted by permission of Pantheon Books, a Division of Random House, Inc.

December 13: Lucy

Lucy died: From *Handbook of Christian Feasts and Customs,* Frances X. Weiser. Copyright © 1952, Society of Jesus of New England, Boston. Published by Harcourt Brace Jovanovich, Inc. Used with permission.

Lucy, whose day: From *The Collected Poems of Thomas Merton.* Copyright © 1968, Abbey of Gethsemani, Inc. Copyright © 1977, Trustees of the Merton Legacy Trust. Reprinted by permission of New Directions Publishing Company.

My candle: From *A Few Thigs from Thistles,* Edna St. Vincent Millay. Published by Harper and Row Publishers.

The Second Week: Rorate Caeli

Master of: From *Souls on Fire,* Elie Wiesel. Copyright © 1972, Elie Wiesel. Reprinted by permission of Summit Books.

Now burn: From "The Wreck of the Deutschland" in *The Poems of Gerard Manley Hopkins.* Published by Oxford University Press.

Be kind: From *The Psalms: A New Translation for Prayer and Worship,* Gary Chamberlain. Copyright © 1984, The Upper Room. Used by permission of the author. All rights reserved.

Chanukah

The lights: From *Gates of the House, The New*

Union Home Prayerbook. Text, "Blessed is the match . . ." by Hannah Senesh. Copyright © 1976, Central Conference of American Rabbis, New York, and Union of Liberal and Progressive Synagogues, London. Used with permission.

The Middle Days

The Middle Days: John the Baptist

The beginning: From the *Revised Standard Version Bible.* Copyright © 1946, 1952, 1971 by the Division of Christian Education of the National Council of Churches of Christ in the U.S.A., as emended in the *Lectionary for the Christian People,* copyright © 1986, 1987, 1988 by Pueblo Publishing Company, Inc. Used with permission. All rights reserved.

On Jordan's bank: Music can be found in *Worship,* #356.

The Spirit: From the *Revised Standard Version Bible.* Copyright © 1946, 1952, 1971 by the Division of Christian Education of the National Council of Churches of Christ in the U.S.A., as emended in the *Lectionary for the Christian People,* copyright © 1986, 1987, 1988 by Pueblo Publishing Company, Inc. Used with permission. All rights reserved.

When first: From "St. John the Baptist" in *Selected and New Poems,* Daniel Berrigan. Copyright © 1973, Daniel Berrigan. Reprinted by permission of Doubleday, a division of Bantam, Doubleday, Dell Publishing Group, Inc.

Hair of the camel: From "Hymn for the Nativity of John the Baptist" in *The Hymns of the Roman Breviary and Missal.* Published by Browne and Nolan, Ltd., Dublin.

O God: Excerpts from the English translation and the original alternative opening prayers from *The Roman Missal* © 1973, International Committee on English in the Liturgy, Inc. (ICEL). All rights reserved.

This is the dead land: From "The Hollow Men" in *Collected Poems 1909–1962,* T. S. Eliot. Copyright © 1936, Harcourt Brace Jovanovich, Inc.; copyright © 1963, 1964, T. S. Eliot. Reprinted by permission of the publisher.

The Middle Days: God's Dream

You must: From *Sir, We Would Like to See Jesus,* Walter J. Burghardt. Copyright © 1982, Paulist Press. Used with permission.

Nothing that: From *The Irony of American History*, Reinhold Niebuhr. Copyright 1952, Charles Scribner's Sons; copyright renewed © 1980, Ursula Keppel-Compton Niebuhr. Reprinted by permission of Charles Scribner's Sons, an imprint of Macmillan Company.

When the great: From *The Gates of the Forest*, Elie Wiesel. Copyright © 1982, Elie Wiesel. Published by Schocken Books.

I fled: From "The Hound of Heaven" in *The Oxford Book of Modern Verse, 1892–1935*. Published by Oxford University Press.

But you have: Excerpts from the English translation of *Liturgy of the Hours* © 1974, International Committee on English in the Liturgy, Inc. (ICEL). All rights reserved.

Hope is: From *Passion of Christ, Passion of the World*, Leonardo Boff, Orbis Books, 1987. Used with permission.

I have: From a speech given by Martin Luther King, Jr., April 3, 1968, Memphis, Tennessee.

O day: "O Day of Peace" (altered) in *Worship*, #654. Text copyright © 1982, Carl P. Daw, Jr. Reprinted by permission of GIA Publications, Inc. All rights reserved.

Father: Excerpts from the English translation and original alternative opening prayers from *The Roman Missal* © 1973, International Committee on English in the Liturgy, Inc. (ICEL). All rights reserved.

There is: Abraham Joshua Heschel, excerpted from *Man's Quest for God*. Copyright 1954, Abraham Joshua Heschel; copyright renewed © 1982, Hannah Susannah Heschel and Sylvia Heschel. Reprinted by permission of Charles Scribner's Sons, an imprint of Macmillan Publishing Company.

Father: Excerpts from the English translation and original alternative opening prayers from *The Roman Missal* © 1973, International Committee on English in the Liturgy, Inc. (ICEL). All rights reserved.

We live: From *The Advent of Salvation*, Jean Danielou, 1962. Used with permission of Sheed and Ward, Kansas City.

THE MIDDLE DAYS: BY JUSTICE AND BY MERCY

The wilderness: From the *Revised Standard Version Bible*. Copyright © 1946, 1952, 1971 by the Division of Christian Education of the National Council of

Churches of Christ in the U.S.A., as emended in the *Lectionary for the Christian People*, copyright © 1986, 1987, 1988 by Pueblo Publishing Company, Inc. Used with permission. All rights reserved.

If you think: From *Souls on Fire*, Elie Wiesel. Copyright © 1972, Elie Wiesel. Reprinted by permission of Summit Books.

Oil, passing: From *Memory of Fire: Volume III: Century of the Wind*, Eduardo Galeano, translated by Cedric Belfrage. Translation copyright © 1988, Cedric Belfrage. Reprinted by permission of Pantheon Books, a Division of Random House, Inc.

Our brokenness: From *The Broken Body*, Jean Vanier. Copyright © 1988, Paulist Press. Used with permission.

A legend: From *Studies in Pharisaism and the Gospel: First Series*. Published by Cambridge University Press.

THE MIDDLE DAYS: HIDE-AND-SEEK

Behold: From the *Revised Standard Version Bible*. Copyright © 1946, 1952, 1971 by the Division of Christian Education of the National Council of Churches of Christ in the U.S.A., as emended in the *Lectionary for the Christian People*, copyright © 1986, 1987, 1988 by Pueblo Publishing Company, Inc. Used with permission. All rights reserved.

You believe: Excerpts from the English translation and original alternative opening prayers from *The Roman Missal* © 1973, International Committee on English in the Liturgy, Inc. (ICEL). All rights reserved.

Because the: From "The Cultivation of Christmas Trees" in *Collected Poems 1909–1962*, T. S. Eliot. Copyright © 1936, Harcourt Brace Jovanovich, Inc.; copyright © 1963, 1964, T. S. Eliot. Reprinted by permission of the publisher.

'To listen': From *Markings*, Dag Hammarskjöld, translated by Leif Sjöberg and W. H. Auden. Translation copyright © 1964, Alfred A. Knopf, Inc., and Faber and Faber, Ltd. Used with permission.

Rebbe Barukh's: From *Somewhere a Master*, Elie Wiesel. Copyright © 1982, Elie Wiesel. Reprinted by permission of Summit Books.

That of which: From *The Sunday Sermons of the Great Fathers*, vol. 1, translated and edited by M. F. Toal. Copyright © 1957, Rev. M. F. Toal, DD. Published by Longmans, Green and Company.

THE EMBER DAYS

But what: From *The Divine Milieu*, Pierre Teilhard de Chardin, translated by Bernard Wall. English translation copyright 1960, William Collins Company and Harper and Row Publishers. Originally published in French, *Le Milieu Divin*, copyright © 1957, Edition du Seuil, Paris. Reprinted by permission of Harper and Row Publishers.

Once two brothers: From *Desert Wisdom*, Yushi Nomura. Copyright © 1982, Yushi Nomura. Reprinted by permission of Doubleday, a division of Bantam, Doubleday, Dell Publishing Group, Inc.

Las Posadas

Las Posadas, literally: From *Posadas, Jornada de María Santísima y San José de Nazaret a Belén*, Celestina Castro, MCM. Published by the Mexican American Cultural Center, San Antonio, 1978.

Divino: From *Posadas, Jornada de María Santísima y San José de Nazaret a Belén*, Celestina Castro, MCM. Published by the Mexican American Cultural Center, San Antonio, 1978.

Las Posadas: From *Fiestas Navideñas*, Trinidad Quintero and Gerald Barnes, eds. Published by the Archdiocese of San Antonio, 1981.

DECEMBER 17

While we: From *The Origins of the Liturgical Year*, Thomas J. Talley. Copyright © 1986, Pueblo Publishing Co., Inc. Used with permission.

Luke shows: From *The Early Christian Fathers*, Henry Bettenson, ed. Published by Oxford University Press, 1969.

When Jesus: From *The Good News Bible*, the Bible in Today's English Version. Copyright © , American Bible Society, 1966, 1971, 1976.

Come, O Feast-lovers: From *The Winter Pascha*, Thomas Hopko, 1984. Reprinted by permission of St. Vladimir's Seminary Press.

O WISDOM

You are: From *Prayers from the Eastern Liturgies*, Donald Attwater. Published by Burns, Oates & Washbourne, Ltd., 1931.

There is: From *The Early Christian Fathers*, Henry Bettenson, ed. Published by Oxford University Press, 1969.

The scribes: From *Letters for God's Name*, Gail Ramshaw-Schmidt. Copyright © 1984, Gail Ramshaw-Schmidt. Reprinted by permission of Winston Press, Inc.

Your voice: From *Hymns to the Church*, Gertrude von le Fort, 1953. Used with permission of Sheed and Ward, Kansas City.

The Creator: From *The Winter Pascha*, Thomas Hopko, 1984. Reprinted by permission of St. Vladimir's Seminary Press.

O mother maiden: From "The Prioress's Tale" in *The Canterbury Tales*, Geoffrey Chaucer.

O Lord: Excerpts from the English translation of *Liturgy of the Hours* © 1974, International Committee on English in the Liturgy, Inc. (ICEL). All rights reserved.

DECEMBER 18

Now the birth: From the *Revised Standard Version Bible*. Copyright © 1946, 1952, 1971 by the Division of Christian Education of the National Council of Churches of Christ in the U.S.A., as emended in the *Lectionary for the Christian People*, copyright © 1986, 1987, 1988 by Pueblo Publishing Company, Inc. Used with permission. All rights reserved.

Now the birth: King James Bible

Mervell nought: From *The Early English Carols*, published by Clarendon Press.

In the psalms: Excerpts from the English translation and original alternative opening prayers from *The Roman Missal* © 1973, International Committee on English in the Liturgy, Inc. (ICEL). All rights reserved.

Joseph: From "The Annunciation" in *Everyman and Medieval Miracle Plays*, A. C. Crowley, ed. Published by J. M. Dent Sons, London, 1956.

Blessed Woman: From *W. H. Auden: Collected Poems*, Edward Mendelson, ed. Copyright © 1944; renewed 1972, W. H. Auden. Reprinted by permission of Random House, Inc.

O LORD

If the lost word: From "Ash Wednesday" in *Collected Poems 1909–1962*, T. S. Eliot. Copyright © 1936, Harcourt Brace Jovanovich, Inc.; copyright © 1963, 1964, T. S. Eliot. Reprinted by permission of the publisher.

The will of God: "Blessed Be the Holy Will of God" in *Treasury of Irish Religious Verse*, Patrick Murray, ed. Copyright © 1986, Estate of Patrick Murray. Reprinted by permission of The Crossroad Publishing Company.

Earth grown old: From "Advent" in *The Pre-Raphaelites and Their Circle,* Cecil Y. Lang, ed. Published by University of Chicago Press, 1975.

I remember: From *Souls on Fire,* Elie Wiesel. Copyright © 1972, Elie Wiesel. Reprinted by permission of Summit Books.

O eternal God: "Prayer of the Incense" in *Eastern Christian Liturgies,* Peter D. Day. Published by Irish University Press, Dublin, 1972.

'Twas in: From *Cambridge Carol Book.* Published by Oxford University Press, London.

DECEMBER 19

There stood: Text translated by G. R. Woodward.

When Gabriel: From *Kontakia of Romanos, Byzantine Melodist. II: On Christian Life,* translated by Marjorie Carpenter. Copyright © 1973, the Curators of the University of Missouri. Used by permission of the University of Missouri Press.

O FLOWER OF JESSE

Adam and Eve: From "He That Should Come" in *Two Plays about God and Man,* Dorothy Sayers. Published by Vineyard Books, Inc., 1977. Taken from *Four Sacred Plays,* published by Gollancz Ltd., London, 1948.

The earth: From *Storyteller,* Leslie Marmon Silko. Published by Seaver Books, New York, 1981.

Vanity of: From *Oxford Book of Christian Verse,* published by Oxford University Press.

Maria walks: Text translated by Theodore Baker.

Hail, O greenest branch: English translation by Christopher Page.

Eve speaks: From *Kontakia of Romanos, Byzantine Melodist. I: On the Person of Christ,* translated by Marjorie Carpenter. Copyright © 1970, the Curators of the University of Missouri. used by permission of the University of Missouri Press.

Regarding: From *Ancient Christian Writers,* translated by James A. Kleist, SJ. Published by Newman Press, 1948. Reprinted by permission of Paulist Press.

DECEMBER 20

Since Adam: From *W. H. Auden: Collected Poems,* Edward Mendelson, ed. Copyright © 1944; renewed 1972, W. H. Auden. Reprinted by permission of Random House, Inc.

Fearful Adam: Excerpts from the English translation of *Liturgy of the Hours* © 1974, International Committee on English in the Liturgy, Inc. (ICEL). All rights reserved.

We do not: From *Cycle of Christ,* Johannes Pinsk, translated by Arthur Gibson. Published by Desclee Company, New York, 1963.

Hail! by whom: From *Days of the Lord,* William G. Storey. Copyright © 1965, Herder and Herder. Reprinted by permission of The Crossroad Publishing Company.

There came: From *Celtic Invocations,* Alexander Carmichael. Copyright © 1972, Trustees of Professor J. C. Watson; copyright © 1977, Vineyard Books, Inc. Used with permission.

The three-fold: From *The Collected Poems of William Butler Yeats* William Butler Yeats. Copyright © 1933, Macmillan Publishing Company; renewed 1961, Bertha Georgie Yeats. Reprinted with permission of Macmillan Publishing Company.

O KEY OF DAVID

Bless earth: From *An Anthology of Old English Poetry,* translated by Charles W. Kennedy. Published by Oxford University Press, 1960. Used with permission.

Good news: From *The Spirit of Christmas,* G. K. Chesterton. Published by Dodd, Mead & Company, 1985.

The Word: From *The Early Christian Fathers,* Henry Bettenson, ed. Published by Oxford University Press, 1969.

DECEMBER 21

Three old men: From *The Sayings of the Desert Fathers,* translated by Benedicta Ward, SLG. Published by A. R. Mowbray and Company, Ltd., 1975.

The justice: From *The Way of the Cross/The Way of Justice,* Leonardo Boff, Orbis Books, 1982. Used with permission.

You have: From *The Collected Poems of Thomas Merton.* Copyright © 1968, Abbey of Gethsemani, Inc.; copyright © 1977, Trustees of the Merton Legacy Trust. Reprinted by permission of New Directions Publishing Company.

There comes: Music can be found in *Oxford Book of Carols,* #90.

O Dawn

As the sun: From *The Early Christian Fathers,* Henry Bettenson, ed. Published by Oxford University Press, 1969.

Every part: Often attributed to a nineteenth-century Native American, Chief Seattle, but actually written in the 1960s or 1970s.

Everything: From *The Divine Milieu,* Pierre Teilhard de Chardin, translated by Bernard Wall. English translation copyright 1960, William Collins Company and Harper and Row Publishers. Originally published in French, *Le Milieu Divin,* copyright © 1957, Edition du Seuil, Paris. Reprinted by permission of Harper and Row Publishers.

By virtue: From *The Divine Milieu,* Pierre Teilhard de Chardin, translated by Bernard Wall. English translation copyright 1960, William Collins Company and Harper and Row Publishers. Originally published in French, *Le Milieu Divin,* copyright © 1957, Edition du Seuil, Paris. Reprinted by permission of Harper and Row Publishers.

Pre-Christian peoples: From *To Dance with God.* Copyright © 1986, Gertrud Mueller Nelson. Reprinted by permission of Paulist Press.

December 22

Mary said: Translation by Gail Ramshaw and Gordon Lathrop, used with permission.

Sing we: Text copyright © 1968, Hope Publishing Company, Carol Stream, Illinois. All rights reserved. Used with permission.

O Ruler

We who: From *Prayers from the Eastern Liturgies,* Donald Attwater. Published by Burns, Oates & Washbourne, Ltd., 1931.

It is our: From *Vatican Council II, The Conciliar and Post Conciliar Documents,* vol. 1, Austin Flannery, OP, ed. Published by Costello Publishing, Inc., Northport, New York. Used with permission.

At the center: From *The End of the Modern World: A Search for Orientation,* Romano Guardini, translated by Joseph Theman and Herbert Burke. Reprinted by permission of Sheed and Ward, Kansas City.

Thou art: From *An Anthology of Old English Poetry,* translated by Charles W. Kennedy. Published by Oxford University Press, 1960. Used with permission.

I begin: From *The Oxford Book of Modern Verse, 1892–1935.* Published by Oxford University Press, 1979.

December 23

Zechariah: Translation by Gail Ramshaw and Gordon Lathrop, used with permission.

Christ climbed down: From *A Coney Island of the Mind,* Lawrence Ferlinghetti. Copyright © 1958, Lawrence Ferlinghetti. Reprinted by permission of New Directions Publishing Company.

To speak: From *Jesus, the Compassion of God,* Monika Hellwig, 1983. Reprinted by permission of the publisher, Michael Glazier, Inc., Wilmington, Delaware.

O Emmanuel

It is both: From *Meditations on Hope and Love,* Karl Rahner, SJ. Published by The Seabury Press, 1977.

On that day: From the *Revised Standard Version Bible.* Copyright © 1946, 1952, 1971 by the Division of Christian Education of the National Council of Churches of Christ in the U.S.A., as emended in the *Lectionary for the Christian People,* copyright © 1986, 1987, 1988 by Pueblo Publishing Company, Inc. Used with permission. All rights reserved.

No one: A homily given December 24, 1978. From *The Violence of Love: The Pastoral Wisdom of Archbishop Oscar Romero.* Copyright © 1988, Chicago Province of the Society of Jesus. Published by Harper and Row Publishers.

The church: Excerpts from the English translation of *Liturgy of the Hours* © 1974, International Committee on English in the Liturgy, Inc. (ICEL). All rights reserved.

The very: Excerpts from the English translation of *Liturgy of the Hours* © 1974, International Committee on English in the Liturgy, Inc. (ICEL). All rights reserved.

December 24

In a flash: From "The Wreck of the Deutschland," *The Poems of Gerard Manley Hopkins.* Published by Oxford University Press.

To cleave: From *The Divine Milieu,* Pierre Teilhard de Chardin, translated by Bernard Wall. English translation copyright 1960, William Collins Company and Harper and Row Publishers. Originally published in French, *Le Milieu Divin,* copyright ©

1957, Edition du Seuil, Paris. Reprinted by permission of Harper and Row Publishers.

Christmas Eve: From *Handbook of Christian Feasts and Customs*, Frances X. Weiser. Copyright © 1952, Society of Jesus of New England, Boston. Published by Harcourt Brace Jovanovich, Inc. Used with permission.

The Lord at: Can be found in *The Oxford Book of Carols*.

Farewele, Advent: From *The Early English Carols*, published by Clarendon Press.

O come: From Antiochian Orthodox Vespers. Used by permission of the Antiochian Orthodox Christian Archdiocese of North America.

Sudden as sweet: From *The Poems of Alice Meynell*, published by Newman Press, 1955. Used by permission of Paulist Press.

It is strange: From *Everyday Faith*, Karl Rahner. Copyright © 1968, Herder and Herder. Reprinted by permission of The Crossroad Publishing Company.

In the last: From *The Church's Year of Grace*, Pius Parsch, translated by William G. Heidt, OSB. Copyright © 1959, The Order of St. Benedict, Inc. Published by The Liturgical Press, Collegeville, Minnesota. Used with permission.

Since the coming: From *The Advent of Salvation*, Jean Danielou, 1962. Used with permission of Sheed and Ward, Kansas City.